Hindutva
or
Hind Swaraj

HINDUTVA
OR
HIND SWARAJ

Translated from the Kannada by
Keerti Ramachandra
with Vivek Shanbhag

U.R. ANANTHAMURTHY

HARPER
PERENNIAL

First published in English in India in 2016 by Harper Perennial
An imprint of HarperCollins *Publishers*

Copyright for the original text in Kannada © U.R. Ananthamurthy
Copyright for the English translation © Keerti Ramachandra and
Vivek Shanbhag 2016

P-ISBN: 978-93-5177-570-6
E-ISBN: 978-93-5177-571-3

2 4 6 8 10 9 7 5 3 1

HarperCollins *Publishers*
A-75, Sector 57, Noida, Uttar Pradesh 201301, India
1 London Bridge Street, London W6 8JB, United Kingdom
Hazelton Lanes, 55 Avenue Road, Suite 2900, Toronto, Ontario M5R 3L2
and 1995 Markham Road, Scarborough, Ontario M1B 5M8, Canada
25 Ryde Road, Pymble, Sydney, NSW 2073, Australia
195 Broadway, New York NY 10022, USA

Typeset in 11.5/14 Cochin Regular at
Manipal Digital Systems, Manipal

Printed and bound at
Thomson Press (India) Ltd.

Foreword

Shiv Visvanathan

People often claim that the age of manifestos is virtually over. They claim that it has been replaced by the expert report replete with information. The classic manifesto combined speech and text to create a political genre. It was as if the manifesto was responding to two traditions, the oral and the written. Manifestos had to be read aloud, declaimed, recited as speech so that one could celebrate the power of voice, and yet, manifestos had to be deconstructed as texts. Between the demands of the hermeneutic and of orality, the manifesto acquired both power and eloquence. There is a textual, in fact scriptural, economy to a manifesto. It would not be more than a hundred pages. It had to be terse, quotable, cryptic, but for all its rhetorical power, it had to be compressed like a crystal in the centrality of the message. The nineteenth and twentieth centuries were the last age of the great manifestos. In fact, one can list among the classical manifestos, Marx and Engels's *The Communist Manifesto* and Mahatma Gandhi's *Hind Swaraj*. One can also think of Thomas Paine's *Rights of Man*. These texts were essentially political. There were also specialized manifestos in art and architecture that proclaimed a new style, a new cult. While the first transformed societies, the second altered disciplines. As a literary form, the manifesto often seems a dying art, to be revived desperately when need arises.

Fortunately, U.R. Ananthamurthy's *Hindutva or Hind Swaraj* signals that the age of the manifesto is not yet over. One of India's greatest storytellers, he chose the manifesto as the genre for his swan song. One needs the speech of manifestos to cut to the very core of Indian politics, the heart of darkness we call the nation state. When Narendra Modi's victory was imminent, an impassioned Ananthamurthy cried out that he would not like to live in an India ruled by Modi. An irked BJP ideologue asked him to leave for Pakistan. Ananthamurthy's answer to Giriraj Kishore and other vociferous critics was this text. His last work was more than a manifesto. It was a prayer, a confession, a plea, an argument, a conversation capturing a world we might lose. Unconsciously, Ananthamurthy, whom we all know most of all as URA, sets it up as a dialogue, an approximation of a play exploring options, choices, outlining the ethical consequences of each political act. It was the last testament of a remarkable man, a storyteller who quietly became the conscience of an era.

There is no doubt that *Hindutva or Hind Swaraj* is a little book written in a desperate hurry, by an author who knew he was dying and yet who understood that the only way to confront death was to affirm life and the living. It is not an exercise in self-pity. It is an attempt to cut to the bone, to state the fundamentals, especially the fundamentals of the state as a regime. It is the testament of a man who refuses to live in a world ruled by Modi. His is not a blanket rejection of Modi, the person or the persona, because no man is alien to him; his is a rejection of Modi's categories, the grids of thinking, the classificatory exclusions practised by the regime. URA becomes a tuning fork of the ethical possibilities of the Modi era. His sense of urgency does not make him topical or journalistic. He reads Modi as a symptom of a deeper malaise. One has to answer Modi in terms of the *longue durée*, of civilizational logic, as part of the challenges India faces in the future.

Ananthamurthy states his methodology clearly. He warns that the dialogic encounter he seeks to develop is distinct from the debates of the ancients, the point–counterpoint of older debates and discourses. He places before the reader two sets of texts, which are roughly contemporary, Gandhi's *Hind Swaraj* confronts Savarkar's writings, and URA contends that Modi is only enacting the logic of a Savarkar script. Modi is thus not an original but merely a mimic, following the logic of a historical position. Ananthamurthy reads Modi as a giant clone, a copy of the original Veer Savarkar. There is an aesthetic of layers in his presentation. It begins from the topical and moves to the philosophical and ethical. Eventually, what he presents is a civilizational response to Modi. He begins by admitting he is confronting a majoritarian regime with hegemonic propensities, and that majoritarianism cannot be the basis of either a rule of law or a rule of reason. In fact, as a repressed unconscious of a collective, majoritarianism can be brutal in its treatment of differences. But what is even more critical is the logic of a majoritarian nation state. It can be demonic.

URA argues that one must challenge the shibboleth that, merely because one has ascended to power through a majority, one can exonerate it from reason. Democracy, he claims, thrives by providing space for the non-majoritarian. Yet he locates such a politics in a wider space as part of an understanding of evil. He realizes that one has to go back to the very notion of evil and explore the evil that lurks behind words like patriotism and development. He notes that a phrase as unpoetic as 'in the national interest' seems to permit any kind of crime or atrocity. URA as poet is measuring the genocidal quotient of words, and especially evaluating the official concepts of the Modi regime, like nation state, development and democracy.

Evil and the Nation State

Evil, as any literary inventor will tell you, summons a Fyodor Dostoyevsky. The Russian novelist understood evil, invented characters who played out the logic of evil, creating a literature which went beyond theology to unfold the nature of ethics. Ananthamurthy argues that one needs a Dostoyevskyan understanding of evil in India but through Indian categories. The evil that haunts India is the new demonology of the Indian state.

To understand evil, one needs a cartographer, a mapmaker who reads signs and concepts, and finds in those indices the seeds of future evil. Ananthamurthy acknowledges the role of political activists Aruna Roy, Medha Patkar and Teesta Setalvad, each seeking to give voice and theory to suffering. He claims that they can recognize evil and serve as warning signs for the future. He literally sees them as the Cassandras of activism.

URA unfolds three moves in his script. Firstly, nature and history, he claims, are being hypothecated in new ways to the state.

For Ananthamurthy, the rituals of evil begin in erasure not amnesia. Amnesia is a poignant forgetfulness. Erasure is the systematic destruction of memories. More than erasure, what makes History obscene is a utilitarian view of history. Ananthamurthy points out that, for Savarkarites, history is an ersatz idea used to fabricate Hindutva. History is useful for the herd. This is why Ganga worship becomes a photo opportunity for the Modi regime; memories need to be mnemonically constructed. One can almost smell an Orwellian department of memory management.

As history is manufactured, there is a cosmos being lost in Modi-land. Development needs not only a false history but a destruction of nature. Ananthamurthy argues that nature is also a form of memory, a world view. Our ancestors, he claimed, knew how to live in harmony with nature. Nature as a chain of being, as a connectivity of worm, soil, seed, ant and butterfly was the guru of farming wisdom. Reading nature was part of the semiotics and hermeneutics of agriculture. Nature was respected and society's gratitude was marked by ritual time. There was a sense of food as the gift. URA talks of the time when alms were available and people survived on weekly meals and generosity. Nature itself was so gracious that the tribal survived on the generosity of nature. The subsistence economy had shades of the commons, of community and sharing. Hospitality allowed for the pilgrim the pilgrim became a commo

URA nostalgically remarks that in the Malnad where he grew up, for the thirsty traveler on foot, who asked for drinking water, there was buttermilk. He moans that those who were generous in the past have now become brokers of development. 'There is no free lunch in a developing economy.'

Artificially constructed history and emasculated nature set the stage for 'development'. With nature destroyed and history hypothecated to the nation state, development as evil can play havoc. Development is the new evil and it is replete with signs. In our times, our shaman claims that evil lies 'in dams, mines, electric plants, smart cities, five-star hotels, hills that were once sacred with tribal gods, towns devoid of sparrows'. URA adds that globetrotters occupy these spaces not knowing where they are. Globalization is the hegemony of non-place.

Development is brand as greed. It is packaged desire. It needs a mask to hide its face, and Modi at election time becomes mask-like. He was the mask of a middle class replete with greed. Modi as a mask was worn by thousands of faces at election time. In the name of need, people voted for. For Ananthamurthy, development is a ritual of seduction through an antiseptic economics. Yet development as salvationism must create its own demonology. The NGO challenging development becomes the mark of Cain for the new regime, especially because it warns India that development cannot tolerate subsistence.

The Nation State as Hubris

URA claims that Gandhi and Godse were dealing with two separate notions of evil. For Godse, evil was external. For Gandhi, evil was encompassed in the textures within. For Gandhi and Tagore, the nation state was the unfolding of evil. For Godse and Modi, it was both God and the ultimate good. However, Ananthamurthy observes that Gandhi also saw the hubris of the nation blossoming in Sardar and Nehru. They were intellectual siblings of Savarkar. There were few differences between them, and those were amplified to set them as 'worlds apart'. In fact, they all suffered from the Napoleonism of nation-building. Such a nationalism, obsessed with the national interest, often abandons the ethics of everyday, he says. The antidote to Savarkar's *Hindutva*, claims URA, lies in Gandhi's *Hind Swaraj*.

For national interest, order becomes the public good. URA points out that it creates a world infatuated by and anxious about terror and anarchy. It was a world captured superbly by the Polish author Joseph Conrad, for whom a world without regulations was a world of evil. His paradigm or model for the public good was the British Merchant Navy with its stern sense of order. There is an implicit suggestion that the heart of darkness might lie in the obsession for order and control. Evil might not be in the heart of the jungle, of anarchy, but at the core of a theory of control or sovereignty as embodied in the nation state.

For Ananthamurthy, good and evil are not – as in Christianity – opposites, but a part of a chain of being. Sin and crime in Christianity remain the responsibility of the individual. In Christianity, sin is Archimedean as you can pinpoint cause and responsibility, while sin in the Hindu vision is ecological. An affront to nature can have an impact anywhere. The crimes of one country can be transmitted to another country by the contagiousness of corporates. This question of evil raises for Ananthamurthy the story of Job. But eventually Job does not concern him as much as Raskolnikov. Dostoyevsky is difficult to shake off. He seems more complex than the Bible. His thought is seminal. A man tired of his bashfulness dreams of becoming a Napoleon just as a society bored with itself wishes to be Rome. 'All evil-minded political leaders dream of matching up to the Roman Empire. Communist Russia and China are victims of the dream.' There is a touch of Raskolnikov in India. One does not need to senselessly murder an old woman as Raskolnikov did. One can equally senselessly, with meticulous logic, murder a minority. Yet there is little of the torment of Raskolnikov. Those deaths only bring to Modi's mind a mongrel caught in the wheels of a car. It is merely vexatious. Guilt and responsibility do not haunt him.

URA argues that the external Modi is a pure figure, a sleepless toiler, an attractive, designed politician, liberated from past and caste. He is an effigy, half Shivaji, half Patel. In Modi, the religion of Savarkar has triumphed in an inflated form.

Modi is not the liberal mind, wondering how to deal with all the vexations: the Dalit vexation, the Muslim vexation, the cosmopolitan vexation. Unlike the liberal, he does not fear he might lose his morality trying to manage these tensions. Such sensitivity is unnecessary for those who manage the nation. Nationalism eliminates its opposites. Like Mao. Like Stalin. Like Napoleon. Like Modi. But there is an alternative to it. An Indian alternative. Gandhi's dream in *Hind Swaraj* was an antidote to all the Napoleons and Modis of history. If Gandhi loses, then Savarkar's history wins.

URA opens with all the power of a fable and the logic of a parable. He knows he is dying and he fears 'the ferocity of the nationalism that lies secretly camouflaged within us'. Ananthamurthy invokes the debate between Gandhi and Martin Buber and remarked that Gandhi was opposed to the creation of a Jewish Israel which banished local people. He adds that the Modi government is a Hindu state on the lines of Israel, and is already aligning with an Israel that embodies a sense of exclusion and machismo.

Modi's victory fascinates Ananthamurthy. He senses it as an act of conspicuous politics, a politics with no sense of introspection. Our prime minister is projected like a hoarding, the nation's collective advertisement and endorsement. He adds there were rituals of electoral victory but no rituals for the dead of Gujarat. The ghosts of the dead haunt none. They became less than mongrels that died under a speeding car. Modi is no Gandhi traversing the streets of Noakhali during Partition. He practices a new raj dharma based on erasure.

To understand Modi, one has to understand Savarkar. URA admits he read Savarkar's *Dark Waters* and admired him as a young man. When he was in London, Savarkar acquired a friend Krishna Varma, who edited *The Indian Sociologist*. The magazine, echoing Spencer, condemned Gandhi's idea of non-violence.

Savarkar borrowed from Hebert Spencer's critique of non-violence. There is a paradox to Savarkar. In building his idea of Hindutva, he summons Western concepts. Yet all he creates is the fabrication of a past devoid of defects. This, says URA, is the first routine step of anyone contriving to build a nation state.

URA's essay blossoms as he compares Savarkar's text with *Hind Swaraj*. The former, he claims, is didactic while *Hind Swaraj* is a conversation with the intimacy of the whispered word. *Hindutva* was intoxicated with the past. For a sentimental intoxication, everything with the past feels fair. But when one reads a text like Vyasa's Mahabharat, it would appear that in the past too, all the attachments, cunning, blasphemy, sexuality, brutality, envy, savagery were there. Savarkar seeks a cosmetic history without pettiness.

Thus URA suggests that India had two models at the beginning of the century. One universalist but localized, the other negating the diversity of religions and languages. Gandhi's vision was of an India of village republics. It could be defeated but never conquered, while Savarkar's narrative engenders brutality through frenzy. An intoxicating history virtually inspires a brutal one. Gandhi's argument is the more self-reflective and critical act. Savarkar's history seeks to challenge power through violence. Gandhi's narrative goes beyond liberation to emancipation. It seeks categories that would avoid the rebrutalization of our societies, seeking to redeem both Indian and British society. Savarkar's was a rationalist reconstruction where religion was not necessary. Gandhi's is a more human endeavor 'where no religion is complete in itself. That is why all religions should survive with equal respect.' Savarkar's idea of nation has a touch of race, of a people from the same stock. Gandhi builds it from the mnemonics and sacredness of space.

URA remarks that Gandhi's *Hind Swaraj* and Tagore's *Gora* are the only foundational answers to Modi. Both show that the answer to a militaristic haughtiness is not moral cowardice, but compassion. A brutalized Modi worshipping a miniature picture of Gandhi is a travesty – just as justifying the pogrom in Gujarat as an act of valour becomes a travesty of the ethical act. Gandhi, not bothered about a sentimental past, challenges the pettiness of present practices. All he wants is the everydayness of good conduct.

URA shows that the Congress is only a weaker variant of Savarkar's ideology. In fact, he notes that Godse saved the Congress from the embarrassment of Gandhi's presence. If Gandhi had lived, the hollowness of the Congress would have been apparent. It pretended to be orphaned by Gandhi's death when it was quietly sighing with relief. Gandhi possessed a truth that needed no militancy, no logic of brutality. Nehru disliked *Hind Swaraj*, which he saw as meshed with villages that, in his opinion, were hellholes of ignorance. He misread the Gandhian village as backward-looking nostalgia.

URA adds that oddly, ironically – and yet logically – Patel, Nehru and their epigoni carried out the logic of Savarkar. None more so than Indira Gandhi. Her Emergency forced the sterilization of Muslims. She gave India the atom bomb. Annexed Sikkim. She was a leader admired by the RSS.

Gandhi's last fasts were an attempt to interrogate nationalism. The hollowness of our civilizational emptiness emerges when we refer to the testing of the bomb as Buddha's smile. There is no enigma here, just the blatant illiteracy and arrogance of a nation state.

The genealogies are clear: Savarkar>Godse>Modi. In fact, in his last speech, Godse asks India to choose between Hindutva and Swaraj, himself opting for the first. For Godse, Gandhi was the brutal pacifist, a man who claimed he could do no wrong. By eliminating Gandhi, he believed he had eliminated a man who had caused the destruction of crores of Hindus.

The choice now is transparent. It is between a unity that allows for discussions, which seeks solidarity across difference on the one hand, and a unity that bulldozes all dissent into uniformity on the other. There is a syncretism here which URA points to. He notes that Christianity and Islam were not successful with their conversions in India. Muslims, to the ordinary Indian, were just another caste worshipping another God. In India, unity in diversity is not a formulaic equation. It is a struggle, a perpetual balancing act. If one is obsessed with unity, diversity is a casualty. If one fusses over diversity, it looks futile. They are paradoxes that URA points out: 'What the Sangh Parivar could not do, Indira achieved. Yet Atal Bihari Vajpayee brought divided India and Pakistan closer to each other.' What haunts India is development. URA claims that if Gandhi were alive, he would have fought development with Sarvodaya.

A Final Thought Experiment

Ananthamurthy's text has an urgency, a hurry. It leapfrogs theologies, histories, civilizations to make a vision of India clear. A storyteller is dying, mortified that India is obsessed with the wrong history. A damaged India needs the therapeutic of authentic storytellers. Memories need to heal, visions need to build and in only a few pages we have a plea, a prayer, and a sacrament for an India decaying inside with development. Development is the cancer of our culture. URA's essay is a shaman's warning to an India moving to self-destruct. He claims that those whom the gods wish to destroy, they first seek to develop. Analyses, memory, nostalgia, ethics, folklore are summoned to this last battle.

The text is scrappy in parts. Often he just floats, outlining argument, sailing literally in summaries. They read like still-lives waiting for a Cezanne to add colour to them. He assembles all to create a last manifesto, a plea, a prayer that India remains the India of memory and his dreams. A storyteller's plea that his world remains alive so that the story can still be told. The original essay has no references, no footnotes, no annotations.

The challenge today is to carry out thought experiments that will confront the axiomatics of the regime. Ananthamurthy's manifesto is a beginning. As trustees of his memory and the values of that world, we need more challenges, dialogues with Savarkar's inflated Dracula. URA would have been content with conversation as drama, happy that the ending was an imagination of new beginnings. A poet cannot hope for more.

（1）

How do I begin this response to the apparent optimism about Modi's election in the media and the public, and my own apprehensions about it?

I am faced with a problem. The Nehru–Gandhi family has been liberated from those flatterers who believed that only that family was fit to rule the country. We have been liberated from them too. Even as I say this, the assassinations of Indira Gandhi and Rajiv Gandhi are tragedies that we must remember. Yet, when it seemed that the nation was delivered from one family, we witnessed an election campaign that resembled the presidential form of electioneering. No south Indian, Assamese, Bengali (in fact, no one from a non-Hindi-speaking state) could have won an election the way Modi did with his loud and rhetorical use of Hindi. A democratic agreement exists between the system essential to create a community, the institutions that preserve law and order, and courts that deliver justice. But by drawing my attention to this and saying that I should accept someone who has ascended to power through a majority because it is the democratic norm is what I don't agree with. For me, providing room for those not in the majority is fundamental to democracy. Therefore, I will speak to you, ignoring those who have denigrated me nationwide for my scepticism about Modi. For the sake of convenient communication, I will present my views in the form of sutras, a set of aphorisms.

• I will start with the story of Job from the Old Testament. Is evil also present along with what we believe is the goodness of the Divine Will? In the 1950s, the visionary author and psychiatrist Carl Jung wrote *Answer to Job*, in which he examines what the Christian world underwent throughout its symbolic history to overcome evil. Similar to this is the Satya Harishchandra story in which Raja Harishchandra is repeatedly tested for his adherence to truth. Can knowing that good and evil are inseparable and exist together, make us aware of the malevolence that might be hiding in our love of the nation?

Every time the leaders of the Modi government open their mouths, they utter the words 'in the national interest'. That is to say, in the 'national interest', one can do anything. Like God. We have a saying: He who gives up pride and shame is like God.

• Let me mention here Raskolnikov, the protagonist of Dostoyevsky's *Crime and Punishment*. He aspires to be a Napoleon – an ordinary man who became a kalapurusha, the man of the age, and acquired glory despite killing thousands in war. The young man is deeply anguished because he could never be like Napoleon, who disregarded commonly held perceptions of evil when he slew thousands in war without guilt. Godse did not think like Raskolnikov. Through his readings of Savarkar, Godse, in his love for Bharat, truly believed that Gandhi, the advocate of non-violence, was an impediment.

• Godse's final speech should be compared with Modi's fervent words of patriotism. When Godse could find no other way to put an end to Gandhi's all-powerful influence in the country, he killed him. The Congress, which somehow managed to obtain nuclear friendship with the

United States, allowed Savarkar plus Modi to occupy the space vacated by Gandhi. Modi has become the true voice of the innate desire for development of the Congress, which is slightly embarrassed by memories of Gandhi. Instead of the gentle satvik[1] face of Manmohan Singh, we see before us the imperious rajasik[2] face of Modi, in keeping with his kshatra[3] traits. This change of face is the result of Modi's successful fuelling of the middle class's obsessive greed. The face of Modi became a favourite of the media during elections, and thousands of his fans flaunted it as a mask. Even so, I voted for the Congress, which had given to the poor the right to information and the right to food. Throughout human history, people have accepted the victory of the victorious as inevitable. This acceptance is born out of the complacency of a comfortable life. In one of Auden's poems the sound of a knock on the door is heard in the dead of night, somewhere in the distance. The comfort that it is far away and not on his street is short-lived. The sound of the footsteps draw nearer and his door is broken down.

Progress should not vitiate the environment. Kayaka, that is work, is essential not only for the body, but for the mind as well, to remain humane. For the hunger that comes from toil, the satisfaction after it is quenched, the simple pleasure that comes from the renewal of everyday tasks, for interaction with those who toil, kayaka is necessary. Machines should be the creation of man's curiosity, an aid to his ability to work, and to increase the fruits of his labour. The yoke, the plough, the spinning wheel, the fuel-efficient clay oven, the tender mango pickle that retains juice in its stalk for several years, the bullock cart, the sewing machine, the steam engine, the bicycle, fire from flint, the paper kite that flies high into the sky, discovering that the inedible-looking dark-grained ragi is in fact the ultimate cereal, the medicinal plants that grow in the backyard – they were all the result of individual and collective effort.

• The right of the poor who make soil and water yield food should not be taken away. Farmers' lands should not be taken away for power generation plants, IT–BT[4] enclaves, mining and five-star hotels. It is to the benevolence of Varuna, the god of water, that we owe the cultivation of food. Before agriculture, humans hunted to survive. Animals were prey, but they were also accorded divine status out of a feeling of gratitude. Hunting hounds became the companions of Dattatreya.[5] The humble mouse became Ganesha's vehicle. The cow provided milk and meat, and in every pore of its body, all the gods were seen. The Westward-looking sky cruisers of today have become heartless hunters, purely traders, without any sense of the sacred. Rich Koreans do not visit historical sites in their own country, they say. I once asked a few North Koreans if the Buddha was sacred to them. The answer was a mockery of Marxism. 'Yes, the Buddhists invented printing and production of books,' said the party-tutored government-appointed interpreter. Only that which is useful is important. In this respect, the capitalists and the communists hold a common view of the ancient past. They are the Benthamite utilitarians. The Savarkarites too use ancient history to instigate and bring together the Hindus. Ganga puja for Modi is a photo opportunity.

• The hunting that corporates do today we call globalization. Those who help in a hunting operation get a small share of the kill, just like we do in the capital market. Those from poor countries seeking IT–BT jobs in foreign lands are viewed as cheap labour that boosts profits.

American universities plan to open numerous educational institutions in India. After all, the ultra-modern, non-smoke-emitting IT industry needs skilled people to run it. The primary objective of these new universities is to develop communication skills and impart a little knowledge of science. This trend isn't confined to the space of technology either. In the past, the art and craft of a place, whether in clay, wood or metal, had its own special skill which told of its origin. Now everything is 'Made in China'. Manmohan's objective was to turn this into 'Made in India'. It has now become the more 'able' Modi's goal. All that should have been made in villages and small towns, as Gandhi had hoped, is now being produced by large industrial units. In the future, buttons will be manufactured by one nation, sleeves by another and collars by a third, and these 'Made in America' shirts will be available in the malls, all of which are replicas of each other – just like the five-star hotels, where it is not hot or cold but controlled air that prevails. Globetrotters occupy these spaces not knowing where they are.

The free time that a farmer gets from his labour allows him the space to appreciate folk arts, music, Harikathe, Yakshagana, and so on.

The leisure for festivals and rituals too is due to the benevolence of Varuna. Farmers who rejoiced when it rained, and anxiously scanned the skies when it did not, knew the cycle of the seasons in their bones. Our ancestors had the humility to live in harmony with nature without teasing it. The butterfly, the ant, the earthworm, the colour of the clouds and the tiny winged insects that take birth to fly for a moment and die – these were the gurus of farming wisdom. On the day of the full moon, Bhoomi Hunnime, farmers offered the earth goddess payasa and partook of it themselves, and felt blessed.

• The MBAs fresh from Harvard, aspiring neo-capitalists, see benevolence as part of a feudal heritage. For these young people populist programmes are a bait in the hunt for votes. Providing food to the hungry at subsidized rates is antithetical to their view of development. Why? The answer is simple. There is no free lunch in a developing economy. The transactions of the local bazaars cannot grow the *market*. Subsidies are harmful to the market.

• In the past, poor students were able to study and become successful because of a practice called varanna. Some Lingayat mutts, religious institutions, also provided free meals for them. Today, this is possible because of the democratic benevolence of reservations.

Tribal communities survive because of the grace of the trees of the forest, the animals, roots and tubers, sunshine and rain; a shared nurturing by large families; the abundantly flowing water; the favour of ragi and jowar that only need to be sowed to thrive. For those who believe in development, these are the impediments of a subsistence economy. It is not conducive to tourism. In the Malnad where I grew up, the thirsty traveller who asked for water was given buttermilk. Nowadays no one travels on foot. There are only tourists with rooms reserved in advance. They have a minister in their service who is of no use to them. The old houses with courtyards and cool floors have all become resorts. Those who were big-hearted in the past have become brokers in this Age of Development.

• However, Medha Patkar, the satyagrahi afflicted with acute back pain, and Aruna Roy, the Right to Information activist, who had tucked in their sari pallus for the big fight have not loosened it still. People like Teesta Setalvad continue to run from court to court seeking to uncover the truth. That they have not given up hope in the present scenario, as the Congress leaders have done, has prevented frustration and dejection from creeping into this writing. I mention this right at the start lest I forget later.

• I attempt to see the evil that is within us and around us in its manifold avatars. The evil of our times are mines, dams, power plants and hundreds of smart cities. Shadeless roads, widened by cutting down trees; rivers diverted to fill the flush tanks of five-star hotels; hillocks, the abode of tribal gods, laid bare due to mining; marketplaces without sparrows and trees without birds.

• If we want development, it is there for the taking. If we don't want it, we can do without it. Corporates, on the other hand, must have development. Because America cannot be polluted. So the poor of India remain silent. And the tribals who have little choice fall prey to the himsavadis, the believers in violence.

• Recognizing that the evil that has tasted power is inside us, and then striving to overcome it is the Gandhian path. Believing that the evil is outside us is the Godse path. Godse was not bothered by the fact that Gandhi was preparing for a prayer meeting. In Savarkar's language Godse was a non-religious believer in the notion of Hindutva. This punyabhoomi, this sacred land, needs Hinduism only as an address. When he killed Gandhi, Godse may not have expected that this great nation, this Bharat would lose its diverse rituals, arts, dresses, cuisines, oils, cereals and become a cheap imitation of Western civilization. Or perhaps he was the seed for the Modi way of the future.

In the world where kshatra dharma prevails (in America, England, China, Russia, among others), the idea of nationalism that Gandhi and Tagore were suspicious of now exists in the guise of multinational corporates. Gandhi's universal brotherhood differs from Nehru's internationalism. 'Development' causes one to forget the past, it belongs to nobody, emaciates the earth, fills the canopy of the sky with smog through which the sun cannot peep, chokes and poisons the flowing rivers, and also boosts a state of excessive irresistible desire – inherent in all of us. Modi, in his short-sleeved kurta, speaking with an uplifted chin, appearing as a dazzling leader, providing twenty-four-hour electricity to corporates, is one of those pushing India towards that hubris. Everyone declares that Modi is not corrupt. That this has become a eulogistic refrain is a tragedy.

• When I was growing up in the pre-war years, we complained that goods 'Made in Germany' were difficult to get, and dismissed as 'Made in Japan' all the shiny cheap items that we actually used. During the war years, German goods were available in the black market. The black market exists even today – in the middlemen who have political patronage. For saying that such people have no place in his regime, Modi has received much praise.

• Today all that glitters is 'Made in China'. America is incapable of manufacturing even a pin or a shirt. What it can produce are weapons of war and supercomputers. Cleverly worded MOUs for development do not require us to stand on our own feet. Instead, we dream of selling pins to the world like China does and to export garments stitched by poor women in sweatshops. The fashion designers who commission these garments are mostly from developed countries.

• NGOs fighting to protect the earth have been declared anti-national. The Modi government is all set to start proceedings against them. Turning a blind eye to the wishes of the southern states, it is constructing a new dam (in Andhra–Telangana), putting the farmers and tribals of the region in a fix. (It was the Congress government that had initiated this project.) In the celebration of Modi's victory, it is clear that India's federalism is being destroyed. The Congress had damaged it sufficiently through its high command culture.

• I would like to compare Raskolnikov, who lost faith in Christ because of his overarching ambition but regained it through anguish and love, with Godse, who recognizing the strength of Gandhi, assassinated him while he was on his way to pray to the Almighty for the well-being of the country rather than his own. Raskolnikov had an inner voice which he despised but could not deny. Godse too may have had it. Born after three male children had died, Godse was brought up as a girl by his parents. Even his name 'Nathuram' meant one who wears a nose stud. But it was not the desire to prove his manliness that made Godse first bring his hands together in greeting, and then shoot the bare-chested old man, the Father of the Nation, walking eagerly towards the prayer meeting, supported by two girls. The act did not need either machismo or plotting.

Gandhi did not even have police protection. The Hindutvavadi Godse's action, committed with utmost detachment and in cold blood, was the sacrificial offering made at the yajna of nation building. And Savarkar's ideology was the text for this yajna. Only in a democratic system does this sentiment, latent in all of us, find expression in the smooth-tongued Modi raising an arti to the holy Ganga.

• When Nehru and Patel formed the government, they followed all the laws of the land but they did not provide security to Gandhi whether he wanted it or not.

• Evil is not evil in the context of love for one's nation. The patriot Gandhi, during his final fast, saw the growing hubris of nationalism in his beloved Nehru and Patel. More on this later. An examination of how Napoleonism gives rise to the desire for nation building, evident in the histories of every country, allows us to understand why Gandhi and Tagore were opposed to the idea of nationhood. Our belief in nationalism leads to a loss of our everyday morality. Raskolnikov couldn't help the presence of this everyday morality in his inner voice. For the sake of an Indian Napoleon, one he believed could build a strong and stable nation, Godse was prepared to kill Gandhi and die himself. This imperative did not come from a morality present in his inner voice but an external rhetoric. Political rhetoric lies to the people; a writer's rhetoric lies to himself, says Yeats.

Godse and Savarkar aspired to a strong system with a mighty army. People like Modi live in a gumbaz, a dome that echoes what they say to themselves over and over again. This in itself is not new for India: the Congress leaders did that too.

• Savarkar believed that only those who view this land as punyabhoomi should rule. Others may only live here. In Modi's government, there is only one woman who does not – according to Savarkar's world view – look upon Bharat as punyabhoomi.

• I will compare Savarkar's analysis of Hindutva with Gandhi's book *Hind Swaraj*. History with its equalities and inequalities, and its highs and lows, has flashes of inner turmoil. My search is for the underlying coherence in it. This writing, born in the current Modi era, should be viewed as an attempt to swim against the tide.

• Like an aphorism, an idea appears throughout this writing, concealed in the light or shadow of several other thoughts. Order is needed, so is punishment – within limits. While extolling the Kodanda (bow) of Rama, who was born to protect the good and punish the wicked, the Kannada poet Adiga expresses scepticism: '*Kodanda dandavu heege danda.*' Punishment is as necessary as it is futile. Ravana's heads grow back as fast as they are chopped off.

• It is important to note that the necessity of order and the inevitability of anarchy are the warp and weft of society. The state and its machinery become redundant and an impediment to our existence, which is made up of a love of life, of our many human relationships and of a self-imposed morality. Goodness is present naturally and effortlessly in sage-like people, in Gandhi and Tolstoy. Gandhi accepted the State but did not embrace it. As a test, Jesus Christ was asked if Jews should pay taxes to Rome. The restrained anarchist replied, 'Render unto Caesar the things that are Caesar's, and unto God the things that are God's.' There is never a time when it is not necessary to oppose the state. That resistance is the ever-essential satyagraha. It is present in the poet's creativity. It is there in the steadfastness of a devotee who confronts his God.

• In his harsh reply to Job's questions, God ignores his own inner humanity. (This trait is present in nation builders like Napoleon, Stalin, Mao and Hitler among others.) Jung examines the phases of God becoming human. Had he known of this vachana by the tenth-century poet Devara Dasimaiyya, Jung may well have quoted it in his book *Answer to Job*:

> He who has a body has hunger
> He who has a body, lies
> Don't blame me for having a body,
> Assume one, O Ramanatha, and then
> you will know.

• This is how the twelfth-century poet Basava sees a mighty king: While a dead rabbit can be seen as edible flesh, the dead body of a ruler is not worth even a single betel nut. For Purandaradasa who lived during the Vijayanagar period, the idea of an ideal state is absurd. I must remember to acknowledge here Ashis Nandy, whose work I read, admired and questioned.

• My essay 'Fear of the Ruler, Fear Without the Ruler' (*Poorvapara*, 1990) was written after Indira

Gandhi's assassination. That is when I began thinking about some of these things.

Several writers and philosophers have been troubled as much by the fear of authoritarian rule as by the fear of anarchic rule. The great novelist Joseph Conrad was fascinated by the widespread anarchy in Poland but was also fearful of it. He found an environment where there were no restraints, no rules unbearable. His ideal was the British Merchant Navy. The harsh rules that the captain of a ship imposes on the crew are applicable to him as well. But within the rigid framework of these rules, there is freedom of creativity for each one. The ship has a life of her own. In English, a ship is referred to as 'she'. Conrad is afraid that man may do whatever he pleases if there are no checks or restrictions on him. To all appearances a rightist, he is an author who believes that man's hubris must not be given free rein.

Gandhi was able to reach his inner God, and heed His words in his fasts, in his silences and in his solitude. His last fast – where he ignored the material benefit to the country for whose freedom he had struggled – was at the behest of his conscience. With this fast he opposed Nehru and Patel, both dear to him. This was possible because of divine grace.

• Man who is a social being, is drawn towards both order and anarchy. This attraction stems from man's goodness. As Adiga says: 'Goodness is not natural. Goodness is not unnatural either.'

• When we say that goodness is not natural, we mean that it is not self-inspired but acquired by learning to lead a life of self-control. Equally true is the statement: 'Goodness is not unnatural either.' That which is not naturally within us, acquired by artificial means, is hypocrisy; it is not the goodness that comes from selfless service. Greed is as much a trait of the self-obsessed individual as goodness is. The state was born to keep him in check. There is a profound Buddhist story that illustrates this.

At the beginning of Creation, food was plentifully spread across the earth like cream on top of milk. Every morning, man helped himself to whatever he needed. It was a time when man did not have to toil for his food. (Give us this day our daily bread.) One day, a man thought: Why should I take the trouble to get my food every day? Why can't I gather it for two or three days at a time? When his neighbour saw this, he also felt that he should stock up as much as he needed for a week. The idea spread, and each one competed with the other to gather more resources for himself. As a result, the generous Earth Mother, who provided enough for everybody every day, ran dry. This alarmed the people and they collectively began to look for an alternative. A Mahasammata[6] was unanimously elected. The people decided to abide by all the rules he formulated. This story illustrates why a state with universally acceptable laws is essential for mankind. It is a story relevant to our times.

• This chaos arises because we believe that the earth is an akshaya patra[7] with limitless resources. (Greed created by development.) The race to scrape the bottom of the akshaya patra begins. Even a man with a conscience is drawn towards it, even as he is troubled by the thought that this akshaya patra could be an illusion. In Marx's view, it is possible to have so much production and progress that the state withers away. For him too the earth is an akshaya patra.

• To understand that man is not all good, nor all wicked, it is not enough to look outside. We also need to see the conflict between good and evil within ourselves. When the outside world is seen through this introspective outlook, we realize how sensitive the state needs to be. To base anything on faith or ethnicity leads to the disappearance of all moral dilemmas in man. When the Western world created Israel by banishing the local people, Gandhi opposed it. Revivalism is not appropriate for history. Gandhi said that the Jews should accept the land they live on and enrich it as their own. This did not go down well with many Jewish thinkers. Even Savarkar must have considered Gandhi a traitor because of his indifference to the nation state.

On a map, Israel appears in the shape of a dagger in the heart of Asia. The Palestinians who are fighting for their land and the Israelis who are trying to contain them with help from America are responsible for some of the turbulence of our times. Islamic terrorists are not hesitant to resort to any kind of violence in the name of the atrocities on Muslims in Palestine. The Modi government, inspired by Savarkar's idea of a Hindu state on the lines of Israel, is clearly aligned towards Israel. Modi, who was like a 'brahma' during the Gujarat yajna, differs from the stand taken by the Vajpayee government.

• The orthodox, whether they are Vaidiks, practising Jews or devout Islamists, will not build a state themselves. But they are necessary emblems for those brave enough to actually do it. The Vaidiks nowadays have become wealthy astrologers reading the horoscopes of politicians.

(2)

In Christianity, not only is there a God, there is also his indestructible rival Satan. In the Puranas, Vishnu's doorkeepers, Jaya and Vijaya, are cursed. To regain their position, they must spend seven lifetimes as God's bhaktas, his devotees, or three as his enemies. Jaya and Vijaya opt for three lifetimes of enmity.

Contrary to this, in Christian folklore, Satan who was banished from Heaven, never gives up his animosity towards God, always waiting to draw us in to the darkness of sin. In the *Book of Job*, Satan provokes God.

'There is nobody on earth who truly loves you. They are all time-servers. They praise you in the good times they have received from you, that's all,' he taunts.

God does not agree. 'There is one man on earth, Job, who has surrendered completely to me.'

'Put him through some hardships and then see if he turns to you or to me,' says Satan.

Then the hardships begin for Job, trouble after trouble. He loses all his wealth. But he does not lose faith. 'You gave it, you took it back,' he says, submitting to God, laying his bare head on the ground.

But Satan is not one to give up easily. 'Take the lives of those he loves and test him,' he challenges God.

Job loses his wife and children. Even then Job goes down on his knees and prays. 'You only took back what you had given me.'

Satan will not relent. 'Job is self-centred. Trouble him further. Then see what he says.'

Job's body is covered with sores. He is groaning in agony. His friends accuse him, 'You must have committed some grave sin, why else would God give you this kind of suffering?'

To Job's question, 'Why should good people who have not sinned suffer, and sinners enjoy happiness and prosperity?', amidst thunder and lightning, Jehovah replies, 'O mortal, accept my Creation without question.'

Then Job asks, 'Is God merciful?', and Christ takes birth as the son of God, personally experiences human suffering and forgives those who have sinned.

Jung examines this tale and asks: If we accept that God is the originator of this universe, then is the evil that is hidden in nature also a part of His divinity?

There is a limit to Christ's mercifulness. On the Day of Judgement, he ruthlessly punishes those who doubt him even though he has risen from the dead. In Rome, there is a painting by Michelangelo in which the compassionate Mother Mary appeals to her son: 'This angry son is not the Christ of before. It is that God who issued Job the stern warning.' Satanhood does not die. The Abrahamic religions have no answer for Job.

There is no Satan in the Puranas. It is Jaya and Vijaya who are the enemies of God, a choice they make in order to reach Him. There is also no one God. As opposed to the Christian practice of one God and one being that defies Him, Hinduism has allotted to the trinity of Brahma–Vishnu–Maheshwara the departments of creation, preservation and destruction. In the Puranas, one could complain about one of them to the other.

To overpower Bhasmasura, who was planning to use the boon he had received from Shiva against Shiva himself, Vishnu took the form of the seductive Mohini. According to Shiva's boon, if Bhasmasura placed his hand on anyone's head, that person would be reduced to ashes. As Mohini danced, Bhasmasura imitated her movements. She placed her hand on her head; Bhasmasura did the same. The boon became a curse. Bhasmasura was destroyed. Then Shiva was drawn to the beautiful Mohini, and of their union, Ayyappa was born. At the end of the Kannada poet Kuvempu's 'Ramayana Darshanam', Ravana has a dream: he is Sita's child.

In a culture that constructs such stories, is it possible to see evil as another facet of divinity? Yes, it is. That is how it has been, through the ages, through the cycles of life. The man who becomes a demon is also part of that life. Worms, insects, birds, lions and tigers, Garuda, Hanumantha, Varaha and Narasimha – in the chain of life, a sin committed by any one creature affects everybody. Arjuna may not have been punished in his own lifetime for setting fire to the Khandava forest[1] and thus destroying the entire serpent world. But Raja Parikshit,[2] his descendant, knows that he will die of snake bite and secures himself in an impregnable fortress. While he is listening to the story of the Mahabharata, the serpent Karkotaka appears in the form of a worm in the fruit he is eating and bites him. Even Rama, an incarnation of Vishnu, is punished for forgetting his raj dharma and shooting an arrow at Vali slyly, killing him. As Krishna, in a later avatar, he is grieving the entire Yadava clan that has destroyed itself in a state of intoxication. The god of gods lies prone under a tree, all alone. That's when Vali, now reborn as a huntsman, mistakes his feet for an animal's and shoots an arrow at him. Krishna dies. What is the relationship between the concept of evil as it appears in the Semitic faith and in the Hindu faith with its principles of karma?

In Christianity, a sinner pays only for his own sins. The Hindu vision is ecological. If one individual commits a crime, all of creation is guilty. Teesta is still fighting against the Gujarat massacre as if she herself was responsible for it. To see whether the violence that erupted during India's Partition remains in him as traces of lust, Gandhi tested himself by lying naked between two young women. Gandhi gave up the experiment because of his disciple Kripalani's censure. An assault on nature in one place is felt elsewhere too – and so the evil of developmental politics results in unbearable heat, bitter cold, ravaging floods, harming the world, here, there, everywhere. Multinational corporations and other industries have the ability to spread, like an epidemic, the sins of one nation across another. The mindless violence that America inflicted on Iraq troubles us even today.

3

In Raskolnikov, Dostoyevsky has created an unforgettable character: an impoverished young man wandering around St Petersburg in tattered clothes, unwashed and unfed. Extremely attached to his mother and sister, the protagonist is mortified that he has to live off their hard-earned money. He borrows some money from a pawnbroker – money that could have bought him a meal – but seeing a man much worse off than himself, the young man gives him the money and walks away.

In that utterly abject, pitiful, penniless state, lonely, but with no desire for friendship, a thought comes to Raskolnikov. Why did Napoleon become great? Because he had the courage to do something big. What is this courage? Winning a battle after slaying countless people and then without remorse preparing for another? Does poor Raskolnikov have this courage?

Through this protagonist, Dostoyevsky presents a novel idea. An idea that is important to understanding human history. Raskolnikov was ashamed of his shyness. His cowardice. His damaged conscience. How could he overcome them? For many discontented young men in Europe of that time, Napoleon had become a hero. Napoleon, who came from a humble background, rose like a rocket to fame and power during the French Revolution. Many people in Europe who celebrated his success were disappointed when he declared himself emperor. Beethoven who had planned to dedicate one of his outstanding symphonies to Napoleon tore up the dedication.

During Stalin's time, that pattern was repeated. To make his Russia like Rome, Stalin constructed imposing palaces with huge domes in Moscow. (I have seen people queuing up for bread under glittering chandeliers there.) The Soviet Union had become a country whose people had nothing to give. All evil-minded political leaders aspired to emulate the Roman Empire. Communism too fell prey to this dream. Even in China.

Napoleon fostered a significant dream in the youth of nineteenth-century Europe. He set out to modernize all of Europe. Our own Nehru writes admiringly about Napoleon, whereas H.G. Wells denounces the emperor, the enemy of his country, both as a historian and as an Englishman.

Raskolnikov thinks about Napoleon too. He has very strong feelings of aversion towards an unpleasant old woman who is a pawnbroker and moneylender. She lives in a narrow lane, in a secure little nest. Raskolnikov thinks that if he can kill her and overcome the guilt, he will know that he has the strength of Napoleon. Obsessed with this thought, he hides an axe under his cloak and knocks on the old woman's door. Cautiously, fearfully she opens the door. Holding out a tightly wrapped bundle, he says, 'Take this cigarette case and give me some money.' While she is trying to unwrap the packet, he strikes her with the axe. He is shocked. He doesn't know what to steal from there. He stuffs whatever is at hand into his pockets.

Just then, the old woman's sister walks into the room. She is described as a meek, submissive and abused woman. Raskolnikov, who had gone there to commit one murder, ends up committing two. This becomes a complex moral dilemma for him. The Christian faith pulls him in, but he does not submit. He despises himself because he cannot become a Napoleon. This symbolic story is necessary to understand the history of Europe.

People like Napoleon who perpetrate unimaginable violence without any sense of shame become heroes in the eyes of the public. Those who are capable of making their country a great nation are like Napoleon. Or like Hitler. Mao's great nation China, which invaded Tibet, is on the same path. For countries where money grows no amount of space is sufficient.

I will attempt to weave in another story with Raskolnikov's. No matter how vehemently Indians declare that we are non-violent, in our movies and our songs we applaud those who come to power through extreme violence. People may practise non-violence in their daily lives but the Indian psyche also admires acts of brutality. Even the names of many Hindu deities would suggest such a reading. Consider the name Murari[1] – one who has vanquished the demon Mura. We do not extol Shivaji for his acts of good governance, but for his skill with counter-offensive tactics. We forget Emperor Ashoka in our political discourse.

It is the same in Europe; perpetrators of violence become rulers. If you go to the Tower of London, you will see that several queens were put to death because they did not produce a male child. Up until now, human history has only recognized heroes who have emerged victorious in battle. We thought that Gandhi's message of freedom through ahimsa heralded a change. Ironically, this ahimsa was fraught with violence too. Streams of blood flowed during the Hindu–Muslim riots. With a staff taller than himself, Gandhi walked barefoot through Noakhali. India celebrated Independence in the absence of Gandhi.

How did Gujarat produce a pan-Indian hero? The Gujarat massacre took place when he was chief minister. To say that he tried to prevent it but failed would mean he was weak. Nobody can say that. One is reminded of an image used by the poet Adiga. When yajnas are conducted, everyone present is involved in some task or the other. But a mantrajnya, an expert in the mantras, does not participate. He is known as the 'brahma', and is crucial to the ritual. The brahma does nothing.

Modi was the brahma. Whatever happened has happened. Raskolnikov was tormented by the thought that he should not have committed the murder. A hapless prostitute teaches him love. Modi also feels remorse. But of another kind. A remorse that says if a pup gets run over by a car, what can be done? One could say, oh poor thing. If the car had stopped, would the puppy have lived?

Here I will dare to express a thought. Maybe this is why the people of India appreciated Modi; see how he silenced the minorities. On NDTV 24x7, Barkha Dutt invites a prominent Muslim and encourages him to praise Modi. We no longer see the harsh-sounding Modi. This is a Modi beloved of all. Who is this Modi created by everyone, including the media?

We are bombarded with images of Modi offering flowers, paying homage to a small photograph of Gandhi. All our apprehensions are dispelled, and what emerges is the image of a new-age leader with foresight, who works without sleep, wears attractive clothes, a turban, holds a mace in his hand – transformed from the outside but unchanged within. He has kept his wife away, he has liberated himself from his past and his caste, has become the new-age Shivaji and Patel. So what if the country is clouded with the smoke of forgetfulness? So what if we forget

Gandhi? Why, we could even erect a statue of Gandhi in London's Westminster if a trade deal is struck.

In the first budget that the Modi government presented, crores of rupees were allocated for a statue of Sardar Patel. I will hazard a couple of guesses about why no one talks about this. First, to set up Nehru as the prime leader, his followers relegated the popular people's leader, Sardar Patel, to the background. Because of that, the Congress is not in a position to oppose the proposal. Second, Modi cannot openly install a statue of his real leader, Savarkar. Although Savarkar was acquitted of a murder charge, his name is sullied. There is a photograph of him in Parliament. That is sufficient for now. In any case, in the development agenda, there will be airports, universities, large buildings and textbooks. Whatever Nehru supporters have done, Modi can do too. Advani may also get a place of honour as a stone statue or a plaque.

It seems to me that the Gandhi era has come to an end; Savarkar has triumphed. Perhaps his victory is transient, but for now he has won. We do not want a Hindu religion with its superstitions, its caste system, its sacred rituals and the like. Let all Hindus unite because the Muslims are united.

We will confront them. Let us create a strong Bharat. This is what Savarkar advocated. He didn't even believe in God. Like Gandhi, he condemned untouchability. Savarkar could interact with Jinnah as an equal. Jinnah was not fettered by religion. Nor was the rationalist Savarkar.

I call Savarkar a rationalist because, for him, what mattered were the factors that unified several states into a single nation. He knew that only if this happened would Bharat gain pre-eminence in the world. We liberals are cautious and view everything with suspicion. We lack the aggressiveness to silence the differences. So some Muslims will keep picking quarrels. As will some Dalits. And the Shudras. Also the cosmopolitan Brahmins. Everyone is constantly engaged in some squabble or other in this great chaos. The problem confronting us liberals is how to resolve these internal quarrels without losing our individual morality and humanism. A tentative, subtle sensibility is, some believe, an undesirable trait in the ruler of a nation.

See how Modi was able to silence the Ambedkarites in Uttar Pradesh. And then pay obeisance to Ambedkar's statue.

See how he put down the Lohiaite-turned-casteist Yadavs. In the future, will the neo-

Brahmins and Manu followers in India's 24x7 media still invite the liberals who have been mouthing the old tiresome clichés? That too when Modi, who can shut them up, is himself from the 'Mandal' caste and the prime minister of the country?

But there is another important fact we must pay heed to. The middle classes, the Shudras, the Dalits and the Muslims have also been swayed by Modi's oratory. They seem to have given up leftist politics in the sway of Modi's honeymoon period. Perhaps it is only the Earth that will speak the leftist language now, battered and infuriated as she is by Modi's developmental agenda. Perhaps she will unleash her fury through the weapons of storms, thunder, lightning, rain, floods and earthquakes.

The liberals, now sidelined, are afraid that the idea of nationhood – if carried to an extreme – can become fascist. There is a good reason for their fear – this was the story of the two world wars. The notion of nationhood is raising its head once again in China too. Our neighbour has given up Mao's policy of popular consensus, turning instead to global capitalism, and has grown quickly and enormously. Stalin drew Soviet Russia into one nation and eliminated all opposition. This is also how the process of change that began with the French Revolution in Europe ended with Napoleon.

He who does not dream is not human. One dreams of the well-being of mankind, a green earth and a clear sky. A dream of Gandhi's ahimsa. A dream where man works for a living, uses the benefits of science wisely and makes sure the environment is not destroyed.

Gandhi's *Hind Swaraj* envisaged such an India. Modi's victory is in direct opposition to that dream. His triumph has moved closer to Savarkar's idea of Hindutva, without actually saying so.

4

When the Great Tao ceased to be observed,
benevolence and righteousness came into vogue.
   Then appeared wisdom
and shrewdness, and there ensued great hypocrisy.

When harmony no longer prevailed throughout
   the six kinships,
filial sons found their manifestation; when the
   states and clans fell
into disorder, loyal ministers appeared.

                  (Poem 18, Tao Te Ching)[1]

I have undertaken a task that is beyond the
present state of my health and the customary
methodology of my study. I am presenting, in
a concise form, two more or less contemporary
texts, one by Gandhiji and the other by Veer
Savarkar. Though my argument may appear

to be in the tradition of the debates of ancient times, it is different. In the turmoil within me, Gandhi sometimes appears to be useless, but he is in fact more relevant today than ever before. I would like to counter Savarkar and Godse who clearly knew that the Bharat that Gandhi desired was very different from theirs. This means confronting the intense fervour of nationalism that lies hidden within us. The inspiration for this modest writing is satvik, not one arising from the aggressiveness shown by Germany or modern China or America.

I feel an urgent need to talk to myself, both because of the nationwide humiliation that came my way when I rejected Modi and because of Modi's overwhelming victory that left me astounded. So also Modi's backing by corporates. And the advertisement-like support given by the media, and how that softened our critical awareness. TV channels we admired for their commitment to the truth actively worked to enhance Modi's public image. They acted in bad faith. While these channels may appear to be suspicious of Modi, they hesitate to criticize him or remind us of the Gujarat massacre. Modi's fluent oratory – in Hindi, which has a pan-Indian appeal, and in a manner that allowed no room for introspection – was among the reasons for his victory. Equally responsible was the corruption in the Congress, the bland and expressionless face of Manmohan Singh, the organizational disarray of a befuddled party that, despite its many achievements, believed there could be no leadership outside the Nehru–Gandhi family, its bankruptcy of intellectual thought, and Rahul Gandhi's unfocused search guided by sentiment rather than conviction. Mesmerized by the visual media, even the sceptics among us turned mere spectators, and are as much to blame.

No funeral rites were performed for those who died in the communal violence in Gujarat. Their ghosts don't seem to be haunting anybody. As our leader Modi calmly says, their death was like that of a puppy run over by a speeding car.

Perhaps the massacre was not at Modi's behest. But I have said it earlier and I repeat it here: Modi, who sat like a brahma at the sacrificial yajna in his cut-sleeve kurta, was transformed into a broad-chested gallant. Modi became the mask that his adoring fans greeted him with wherever he went. Like Krishna in the Ras Kreeda,[2] Modi was everywhere.

There is another matter to note. In our society, casteism is home to envy not hatred. But the historic mistrust of Muslims can flare up at any time. The dazzling eloquence of development concealed this. For Modi emerged from the Gujarat massacre with the aura of a leader who brought the Muslims to their knees – in spite of the fact that the Supreme Court pronounced him not guilty.

Modi has brought communal harmony to Gujarat in two ways. After the Gujarat bloodbath, a socialist-turned-Hindutvavadi friend said to me candidly, 'What happened was unfortunate. But as a result, the Muslims will be subdued. It is in their own interest.' Another respectable perspective: 'Look, in Gujarat alone, there have been no Hindu–Muslim riots after that painful episode.'

Prime Minister Vajpayee advised Modi to follow raj dharma.[3] However, he himself forgot this at the Goa Sammelan held a few days later. All these thoughts, useless as they seem at this moment, are the reason for the feelings of unease and for my grumbling.

It is difficult to say how genuine this feeling of guilt is. It is said that while Gandhi, with a staff taller than himself, walked the streets of Noakhali, clearing them of excrement and shattered glass, to protect the lives of Hindus, slept naked between his companions he often woke up in the middle of the night and paced up and down, wringing his hands, muttering to himself, 'What shall I do? What should I do?' When there are instances of mob violence, unlike Christ or Gandhi, we do not take personal responsibility. Nobody is punished. It has become a tool in the hands of honourable politicians to use people for their own selfish ends. This is also true of the killings of Sikhs by some wicked Congressmen after Indira Gandhi's assassination. Nobody was punished – neither Hindus nor Muslims – for the senseless killings during Partition. Riots are a quick way of teaching innocents a lesson.

5

In the first two decades of the twentieth century, some eminent Indians who lived in England, several Indian intellectuals and a few young men not afraid to sacrifice their lives were engaged in conceptualizing a vision of an independent India. During the first War of Independence, which the British termed Sepoy Mutiny, Hindus and Muslims were not enemies.

With their divide and rule policy, the British divided us into mutually mistrustful factions. On the level of individuals, the two communities live together by a moral code that builds trust. However, when we are incited, we become a faction. Factions have no soul, no mind. Hindus and Muslims started living as separate communities, in their own areas, not eating together, not playing together.

As a young boy, I became an admirer of Savarkar after reading a translation of his Marathi novel *Kaale Pani* (Dark Waters) and hearing about his daring acts. I had heard about his thoughts on the principles of Hindutva. But I had not read *Essentials of Hindutva*, which he wrote in 1921–22 while in prison. As someone who wants to question Modi's ideology, I needed to find the roots of that particular aspect of Modi's personality which could be present in all of us, in our subconscious. I have not fully read Savarkar's much-acclaimed *The Indian War of Independence 1857*, which refutes the British claim that it was a mutiny by the sepoys. In this book, he expresses trust and admiration for the Muslims. His attitude changed subsequently – it would be wrong not to point this out.

In London, Savarkar had a friend, Krishna Varma, who was an acquaintance of Gandhi's. In 1906, when Gandhi went to London, he stayed with Varma and discussed swarajya with him. Varma used to edit *The Indian Sociologist*, a journal that argued that Spencer's ideas were important for the modernization of India. Its cover page quoted two lines from Spencer. One was: 'Every man is free to do that which he wills, provided he infringes not the equal freedom of

any other man' (*Principles of Ethics,* Section 272)
The other was: 'Resistance to aggression is not
simply justifiable but imperative. Non-resistance
hurts both altruism and egoism' (*The Study of
Sociology,* Chapter 8).

Like Gandhi, several Indian thinkers were
drawn to this journal. However, around 1909,
serious differences of opinion arose between
Gandhi and Varma. The October 1913 issue
of *The Indian Socialist* denounced Gandhi's
principles of ahimsa on the grounds that
these principles of ahimsa create a fear of the
moral, political and social ideals within us, thus
destroying them. While Krishna Varma was
very good at bringing together expatriate Indian
revolutionaries, Savarkar was the brain behind
the movement.

Savarkar had received the Shivaji scholarship
from Krishna Varma, and was encouraged by
Bal Gangadhar Tilak in his endeavours. Savarkar
had been living in India House since 1906. He
was arrested for his revolutionary activities in
1910 and sent to the Andaman Islands. While in
London, he published two books in Marathi, *The
Life of Ghazni* and *The Indian War of Independence
1857.* They were later translated into English.

Gandhi knew about the discussions around these two books. Madan Lal Dhingra (1883–1909), an engineering student at the time, was one of Savarkar's staunch followers. In an act of misplaced bravado, he killed Sir William Curzon because Savarkar's ideas had led him to believe that it was a revolutionary act. We are reminded of terrorists who are willing to kill themselves. This murder was a matter of much public discussion at the time Gandhi visited London. It was described then as 'terrorism influenced by nationalism'. Gandhi writes to his friend Henry Polak about this incident: 'Mr Dhingra's defence (by Indian revolutionaries) was inadmissible. He was egged on to do this act by ill-digested reading of worthless writings. It is those who incited him to this that deserve to be punished.'

The Indians in London believed that Savarkar encouraged Dhingra to commit this crime. Gandhiji met Savarkar in 1909 and participated in a lecture meeting with him. The topic of discussion was: 'Does the Valmiki Ramayana instigate violence or non-violence?' Both of them expressed their opposing viewpoints quite candidly.

Gandhi wrote: 'Contrary to my understanding, Krishna Varma and Savarkar believe that the Gita and the Ramayana advocate violence.' Based on all this, some people think that Savarkar was the inspiration for Gandhi's *Hind Swaraj*. The voice of the respondent in *Hind Swaraj* could be Savarkar's. In London, Savarkar promoted Hindu–Muslim unity. Later, in his book on Hindutva, he took a completely contradictory stand. It is no surprise that one of his leading disciples went on to kill Gandhi. Tolstoy had supported Gandhiji's ahimsa in one of his letters, in *Letters to a Hindoo* (1908) [See *The Collected Works of Mahatma Gandhi*, Vol. 10, pp. 242–44]. This letter was strongly condemned by one Chattopadhyay in the journal *Vande Mataram*. I have collected some of these details from a bold and intense book by Anthony J. Parel (*Gandhi: 'Hind Swaraj' and Other Writings*, Cambridge University Press, 1997). I would like to quote from it:

'Tolstoy argued that non-violence is the only legitimate means available to the morally upright conscience. Gandhi, in *Hind Swaraj*, supported this view while expatriate moderns such as Das and Chattopadhyay opposed it.'

6

In this chapter, I try to distil the essence of Savarkar's book, in my words as well as Savarkar's own. I start with his:

'Inscribe at the foot of one of those beautiful paintings of "Madonna" the name of "Fatima" and a Spaniard would keep gazing at it as curiously as at any other piece of art; but just restore the name of "Madonna" instead, and behold his knees would lose their stiffness and bend, his eyes their inquisitiveness and turn inwards in adoring recognition, and his whole being get suffused with a consciousness of the presence of Divine Motherhood and Love! What is in a name?'[1]

Savarkar uses this example to explain the difference between 'Hindutva' and 'Hinduism', and states that we must use the word 'Hindu, just as the painting should be referred to as Madonna. Hindutva, he writes, is a word that

49

brings to mind all of our history, while the suffix 'ism' denotes an ideology or opinion. Savarkar's description of the Hindus who came to the Indus Valley in the ancient times and performed their rites and rituals there is fascinating. He believes that the great truths that came to them in that period were powerful enough to build a major civilization. In writing this, Savarkar uses several European ideas to support his arguments. He also appears to appreciate Shakespeare.

He praises India of Vedic times as a land of seven rivers (Sapta Sindhu). The intense love for the seven rivers is evident here. To appreciate the meticulousness with which Savarkar derives the etymology of the word Hindu, one must read his book. Objective historians like Romila Thapar are better placed to examine how historically true this is. I do not understand it fully, it is beyond the scope of this book, and the subject itself is significant enough for another essay.

Savarkar goes on to discuss how the Hindus spread from the Sapta Sindhus. Sacrificial fire was a sacred symbol for them. Empowered by this fire, they cut down forests and established towns and turned towns into kingdoms. As these people began to identify themselves as Kurus, Kashis, Videhis and Magadhis, the word Hindu gradually faded. And yet their aspiration to build a nation is evident from the use of the word 'chakravarti' (emperor). Savarkar writes that the Hindus conquered Ceylon. After winning many battles, the Ceylonese acknowledged Ramachandra as a chakravarti. The Aryan leaders also took into their fold non-Aryans, with names like Hanuman, Sugreeva and Vibhishana. Aryans and non-Aryans were partners in those nation-building wars. This was the dawn of our nation, he declares. In fact, the evolution of a country into a nation is the inspiration behind Savarkar's writing. Unity, therefore, is of prime importance to him. For Savarkar, diversity is the result of a misconception. Or, as the Hindutvavadis of today believe, Unity in Diversity is a Nehruvian concept.

Savarkar does not wholly accept the concept of 'Aryavarta', the land of the Aryans. Because when the Hindus were a nation, even non-Aryans were part of it, and this fact is important to him. Remember, Savarkar's thoughts were focused on how India could become a supreme nation. When Hindus spread to the south, the word 'Bharat Khanda' (Indian subcontinent) was born. Savarkar quotes the *Vishnu Purana*, 'The land which is to the north of the sea and to the south of the mountain Himalaya is called Bharat by Bharata's descendants.'

Savarkar did not believe in the supremacy of the priestly class either. 'Will we become a nation of "mlechchhas" if the caste system is destroyed?' he asks vehemently. Some sanyasis, the Arya Samajis and the Sikhs, among others, rejected the varnashrama dharma.[2] Savarkar asks: Aren't these our people? If a country is to become a nation, should it not have a language? The medium of communication across India has been Hindustani. Sadhus and holy men managed to get by with Hindustani as they traversed the length and breadth of the country, he says.

Just as it had happened throughout history, India too had become complacent in its prosperity. It weakened because it lived in a world of dreams. The region was awakened by Muhammad of Ghazni's invasions. Thus began its struggle for survival. In such conflicts, questions of identity and self-awareness arise. When Ghazni the idol breaker attacked our country, all of India could have united. (The word Ghazni was invoked to put fear into us when we were children.) But the Muslim invasion did not affect the people of this country greatly. The civilizations of Egypt, Syria, Afghanistan, Baluchistan, Tartary, Granada, right up to Ghazni, all fell to the Islamic sword. This sword wounded India too, but did not destroy it. With every blow, the sword was blunted. The life force of the victim proved to be more powerful than the strength of the victor.

Savarkar, while he says that this is not only India's story but that of all Asia, does not believe in the coexistence of multiple cultures.

To establish the pre-eminence of India, Savarkar compares it to other nations. The Arabs could not protect their own land. In India, the Arabs, Persians, Pathans, Baluchis, Tartars, Turks and Mughals fought with each other. Religion is a powerful force, and so is rapine. Together the two could create unbearable suffering and barren wastelands. Is this what happened to India under foreign rule?

To ask this is to take a squint-eyed view.

Savarkar also claims that Hindutva won a moral victory during Akbar's reign and during Dara Shikoh's time; Aurangzeb's innumerable efforts to curb the Hindus failed. The Hindus lost the Third Battle of Panipat and yet they won. No Afghan could invade India after that. The Hindu flag held aloft by the Marathas motivated the Sikhs to march up to the borders of Kabul. In this battle we came together as a nation as never before, says Savarkar. Sanatanis,[3] Sikhs, Aryans, non-Aryans, Marathas, Madrasis (a word Savarkar used), Brahmins and Panchamas[4] – they all lost as Hindus; they also won as Hindus. Therefore, to him, Hindustan was a more powerful and acceptable term rather than Aryavarta, Dakshinapatha, Jambudweepa or Bharatvarsha.

Savarkar writes that nobody has dared to critically examine the period between AD 1300 and 1800. With greater feeling he declares: 'The Malabari Nairs mourned the plight of the Kashmiri Brahmins.'

Savarkar bases his arguments on several Hindi poetic texts. One such epic poem is Chand Bardai's 'Prithviraj Raso'. Another poet he invoked was Samartha Ramdas.[5] Also, Kavi Bhushan[6] who challenged Aurangzeb through his writing, and was a great admirer of Shivaji, even though he was not a Maratha.

The Hindu empire that Savarkar describes collapsed in 1818. He goes on to talk about how the idea of the Hindu was sullied by our enemies and made distasteful for us. Hindu is not a black man as the enemies believed. The Hindu religion is all-inclusive and all-encompassing. He quotes a line: *'Shiva Shivah na Hindu na Yavanah.'*[7] With the passage of time, some concepts tend to get corrupted.

To illustrate this, Savarkar gives this example: The Norman who conquered Britain was insulted when he was called an Englishman, but England did not care to change its name to Normandy after the conquest.

I have reservations about how Savarkar paints the word Hindutva with the power and glory of kshatra in a highly emotional manner. In the process of establishing nationhood, all countries draw pictures of a flawless past. We can view our past with its many joys and sorrows without exaggerating them. The Upanishads and the Mahabharata can thrill us. When one looks at the heroes of the Puranas – performing animal sacrifices, and destroying forests, animals and birds to establish a country – one can only wonder, in bemusement, whether they are not champions of modern development. But the nationalist Savarkar did not see a world like the one he lived in, suffering and struggling to overcome the humiliation of British rule. Instead, he saw a glorious, mythical, unique world to be emulated exactly.

The truth of life is different. For Buddha, who lived in ancient times, life was full of suffering. A seeker of truth must, like Gautama, see a corpse, an old man and a sick person groaning in pain. In his search for the truth, he must renounce the world and then come back to it.

Two important events from our past are Dharmaraja's sorrow after his victory in the battle of Kurukshetra and the anguish and compassion that liberated Buddha, making him relevant even today. Savarkar's line of thought could generate in us the daring to kill our enemy, but it cannot satisfy us. The coronation of Sri Rama is a golden moment in our mythology. That's all it is. We take pride in it. To be liberated, though, we need the Upanishads and Buddha.

Savarkar's emotion-charged logic flows in this manner: If India is to be a Hindu state, if all citizens of the country are to be considered Hindus, when will we be able to call a Muslim a Hindu? Maybe at some later date, not now. At the time when this idea becomes a reality, there will be no arrogance amongst the religious. The followers of religion will give up their arrogance and live in harmony, a state which is natural to human beings. Or religion itself will become irrelevant.

Contrast this with what Gandhi says: No religion is complete in itself. That is why all the religions of the world should survive. With equal respect.

Savarkar warns us not to forget the harsh truths of the present day, even though mankind may unite one day in the future. Suppose an American becomes an Indian citizen, he will be one of us. However, until he accepts our culture and history and worships Hindustan, he will not become a part of the Hindu family. Savarkar's idea of nationhood is very similar to that of Europe's. There is a flavour of fascism to it. Hindus are not the citizens of India only because they live together and are united in the love for their motherland. More important is the fact that they are blood relations. They are not just a nation, they are a race. (Savarkar uses the word 'jananga', race. He derives this word from the root 'jan' which means to be born.) Everybody is related, all are from the same stock; all Hindus share blood ties. In the 'Pratisarga Parva'[8] of *Bhavishya Purana*,[9] the poet refers to the land of the Aryans as Sindhusthana. And those outside it are called 'mlechchhas'.

Although Buddhism is a world religion, it did not have an affinity with one land, so it could not be a base on which our nation could be built.

Savarkar says, 'It pains me to write thus about the Buddhists.' Why does he reject Buddhism?

He says it is political. Though the Buddhist Sanghas are sacred to the world, it was necessary for him to give them up, he says ruefully. 'While thy words are gathered from the lips of gods, my ears and my understanding are trained to the accents and the din of this matter-of-fact world. Perhaps it was too soon for thee to sound thy march and unfurl thy banner while the world was too young and the day but just risen!'[10]

Savarkar goes on to state: 'Immobile forces are the easy prey of the mobile ones; those with no teeth fall a prey to those with deadly fangs; those without hands succumb to those with hands, and the cowards to the brave.'[11] Savarkar worships Buddha. But from a distance. It is Shivaji he holds in close embrace. Whenever Savarkar talks about defeat, he does not fail to mention that Hindutva remained undefeated. Although we lost at Panipat, Nana Phadnavis and Mahadaji Shinde lived to fight for forty years more.

Savarkar is obsessed with delving into the origin and meanings of the word 'Hindu' – an exercise that often appears needless. So what if the word does not occur in Sanskrit, he repeatedly asks. He persistently attacks those invisible enemies who object to the use of the word. He does not stop at saying that for a state to become a nation, it needs a language, an oral history, a uniform religion. He goes on to assert that civilization is the overcoming of the material world. The more divinity a civilization imbibes, the richer it is. In this way, sentiment is mixed with political expediency. Knowingly or unknowingly, Savarkar adds a sheen to his politics when he says that his arguments are deeply philosophical.

Another important thing Savarkar says: 'There are some who say Hindus have no history. Actually, it is only the Hindus who have preserved their history.' We are a Hindustan, he declares. The Bengalis speak about the defeat of Prithviraj. The Maharashtrians talk about the martyred sons of Guru Gobind Singh. A south Indian Sanatani mourns the death of Guru Tegh Bahadur who, he believes, died for him. Ashoka, Bhaskaracharya, Panini, Kapila make us thrill with pride. If nothing else the Ramayana and Mahabharata unite us into one nation. The impassioned Savarkar marches forward enthusiastically.

Have we not had internal battles, Savarkar asks, and then replies: Haven't England, Germany and America faced similar strife? Savarkar's view is that Sanskrit is our common language. His Hindu thought, in fact, derives its strength from its base in Sanskrit.

Savarkar also writes about festivals common to all faiths. He believes that the Bohras and Khojas have Hindu blood ties. He rejects the notion that only those of the Vaidik faith are Hindus. For him, a Hindu is not only he who practises Sanatana dharma based on Shruti and Smruti as in the Puranas but also the Sikh, the Jain and the Buddhist.

In this Hindu state are all the rivers, the valleys, the mountains, the evening shadows and the hardships of everyday life. The philosophies of Buddha and Shankara incorporate the essence of it all. In a state of high emotion, Savarkar says that Ram was here, Krishna was here, so was the Bodhi Vriksha. The Muslims converted and did not subscribe to these sentiments, and so he considers them outsiders. Hindustan may be their motherland but not their holy land. Their holy land would be Arabia or Palestine. Although sects like the Bohras have some attributes of Hindutva, India cannot be their holy land. To be recognized as a Hindu, it is not enough for India to be only a motherland, a matrubhoomi. It must become the holy land, punyabhoomi, as well. Hindutva does not mean Hindu religion. Similarly, Hinduism is not Hindu religion alone.

He poses a difficult question. Can Sister Nivedita be called a Hindu? Perhaps. But she did not have the blood ties that Savarkar mentions. If someone like her married a Hindu, she would have acquired blood ties. But since Sister Nivedita was a sanyasini, this was not possible. In spite of that, because she embraced our culture and our country as her punyabhoomi, Sister Nivedita became a Hindu. On the basis of this unique example alone Savarkar expands the scope of the word Hindu. From what he says, the yardstick for judging who is a Hindu should not be too rigid. But it shouldn't be too flexible either.

Savarkar says every country must have its own core community. Take Turkey, for example. The Armenians and the Christians dissociated themselves from Turkey. Or, say, America. When the war started, the Germans distanced themselves. The Blacks identify with Africa. So in the end, the power of America rests on its Anglo-Saxon population. Similarly, Savarkar declares, the Hindus make Hindustan.

7

My summary of Savarkar's book does not capture his fervour, but in fact he writes with immense conviction and passion. Savarkar's world view was bolstered by the words of Lokmanya Tilak whose faith in Hinduism was not just emotional but tempered with wisdom, and the sharp and sensitive Bengali litterateur Bankim Chandra Chattopadhyay. Even Alur Venkatarao, who led the Unification of Karnataka movement, says that he felt a greater admiration for Tilak than for Gandhi.

This attraction for Tilak or Bankim does not appear to have violence inherent in it. Even today, Bankim's composition 'Vande Mataram' gives me goosebumps. In the third stanza of the poem written by Tagore, whose first stanza is our national anthem, there is a line that has a breadth of vision. It describes India as a beautiful path with rise and fall.

If I had read this book by Savarkar as a naive eighteen-year-old admirer of Vivekananda, I might have been confused. I had liked *Dark Waters*. All freedom fighters, regardless of their differences, were the same to me. At that time, I was growing up in an agrahara where there were constant debates on dvaita (dualism) and advaita (monotheism). I was besieged by certain doubts. Before taking the ryots[1] to court for not paying their dues, the zamindar would make a complaint to a bhoota, the lowest of local spirits, or at the temple in Dharmasthala. This would frighten the ryots. My father, who worked for a Brahmin mutt, was greatly pained to see the numerous cases that landlords filed against the ryots. He himself never went to the bhoota to make complaints. I remember my father had a friend who used to collect the tax on behalf of Dharmasthala. On one occasion, some ryots were unable to pay their taxes, and were afraid. The agent from Dharmasthala came to my father to find out how to file a case against them. My father, with a lawyer's shrewdness, gave him some sage advice: 'There is a system here of collecting tax by invoking the fear of Bhootaraya. If you go to court, people's faith in Bhootaraya will be damaged. Keep this in mind before you decide to go to court.' My father belonged to the Vaishnavite Madhwa sect, and believed that Sri Hari was the only deity that could rule us. Shankaracharya was, for the Veer Madhwas, an incarnation of the demon Manimantha.

The hallowed court at Dharmasthala protected the code of ethics that governed our day-to-day lives. People were afraid to swear in the name of Dharmasthala. Once, a complaint was made at Dharmasthala against my father and he received a summons. My father, who interacted with the government and the courts in all his worldly affairs and had implicit faith in B.R. Ambedkar's Constitution of India, tore up the summons in front of me.

This was also roughly the time that Shantaveri Gopala Gowda, Basavani Rama Sharma and Aithal formed the Ryot Sangha and instilled in the ryots the idea that it was better to go to a court of law and depend on satyagraha rather than leave matters to God and the spirits. So God became for me someone who poked his nose into minor affairs. The same faith in God that was used to punish people would send them into a trance, and make them dance holding a singara (bunches of green leaves and flowers) in their hands. I would watch them with trepidation. These rituals also gave me a strange thrill, though. I was afraid that when the spirit Panjurli[2] danced before me, I too would be possessed. I would hold my breath and try to keep my balance. But there were some who came under its influence and began to dance in a frenzy.

I didn't see anybody identifying themselves as Hindu when I was young. The word Hindu is the means to overcome false pride in one's caste.

In my search for God and my desire to become Vivekananda, I would sit atop a hillock chanting the Gayatri mantra. But when I went to Tirupati for my upanayana ceremony and saw the bejewelled and bedecked deity Thimmappa, I felt he was not a god at all. Anyway, who am I? People like Basava and Kabir, who put themselves through a rigorous search for divinity, exhausted themselves, were renewed, and experienced the formless Brahman. Yet, they were sceptical.

Savarkar was compulsively excessive in his expression and approximated profundity through impassioned writing in *Hindutva*. I cannot help but compare and remark that Gandhi's writing during his youth was constructive as opposed to this. In the use of language the difference between Savarkar's fluency and Gandhi's subtle and restrained manner is to be noted.

Nationalist ideas never die. In conducive circumstances they raise their heads like mushrooms after the rains.

8

Savarkar's writings were in opposition to Gandhi's principles of ahimsa.

Let us then examine Gandhi's *Hind Swaraj*. This reflective reading is not only a lens on the current times, but it also highlights our deep aspirations that appear to be defeated for now. I am convinced that thoughts don't die. Before Gandhi came Tolstoy, Ruskin, the *Kathopanishad*, the Gita, the Ramayana and the Gujarati poet who wrote '*Vaishnava Jana To*'. I have read *Hind Swaraj* in several editions. But the excellent version edited and annotated by Anthony Parel,[1] a professor at the University of Calgary, was key to my own understanding of the text.

Gandhi wrote this book aboard the SS *Kildonan Castle* between 13 November and 22 November 1909 while returning to South Africa from England. All of it was, in fact, written on old paper he found on board. If he got tired of writing with his right hand, Gandhi used his left. Forty of the 275 pages were written with the left hand. He did not make many changes to the original manuscript, other than to strike out no more than sixteen lines and change a few words. Some people compare *Hind Swaraj* with the book Rousseau wrote during his travels. Hermann Kallenbach, a friend of Gandhi's, was the first to read the manuscript.

Gandhi originally wrote the book in Gujarati and then translated it into English. The British government banned the Gujarati version, but not the English one. It is worth noting here that Gandhi reached out to his own people in Gujarati and to the whole world in English. Tolstoy and the French writer Romain Rolland, Nehru and Rajaji have all commented on this work. *Hind Swaraj* was the seed. Gandhi grew a tree out of it. Parel compares it to Rousseau's *Social Contract*, St Ignatius of Loyola's *Spiritual Exercises* and the *Gospel According to Matthew*.

Hind Swaraj is a very special text: despite its name – Indian Home Rule – Gandhi's treatise seeks to liberate not only India but also Britain from the yearning for modern civilization.

There is a significant difference in the way Savarkar and Gandhi wrote. Savarkar addressed his readers in a tone of heightened emotion. Gandhi spoke to them in an intimate manner. It is important to note that Gandhi's work is in the form of a dialogue. Our ancient texts used a similar format, where the opposing viewpoint was set up as an adversary's and then dismantled through argument. But Gandhi's book does not do this. While one viewpoint is presented in opposition to another, the tone and tenor is that of a dialogue. In his writing, Savarkar sounds like an orator, addressing a large Hindu community so that they forget their flaws and swell with pride in their love for their nation. However, Gandhi's words are spoken in confidence, as if he speaks to just one listener. The speaker (Gandhi) reminds readers who are hasty in their thinking that, in India's freedom struggle, those who appeared slow movers were the ones who showed them the path of truthfulness.

They call Dadabhai Naoroji the Grand Old Man of India. He was the first to plough the Indian soil. Had it not been for him, we would not have had the words 'Home Rule' to use. There were also a few eminent Europeans at the time, like Hume and Sir William Wedderburn, as well as Indians like Gokhale and Justice Tyabji whose views were important to Gandhi. To the himsavadi reader who may be prone to violence, Gandhi says that there were many Englishmen too who loved India. 'Home Rule' may appear to be a dream, he says, and quotes a proverb to reassure the reader: 'A tree does not grow without a seed.'

Gandhi gently warns us not to ignore the efforts of the early freedom proponents. He earnestly persuades the reader that Dadabhai Naoroji was the first to point out that the British sucked our blood. If one rung of a ladder is removed, he asks, wouldn't the ladder be rendered useless? If we go beyond our guru's teachings or advice, do we render our foundation weaker? Gandhi praises the ideas and contributions of Gopal Krishna Gokhale. He objects to the harsh criticism of Gokhale that appeared in Lokmanya Tilak's newspaper *Kesari*.

If all Englishmen were viewed as enemies, Home Rule could be further delayed, Gandhi fears.

At the time that Gandhi was writing this tract, there were two opposing groups in India: the Moderates and the impatient Extremists. Those who believed that our country should gradually work towards freedom were dismissed as moderates. The mahanayak or grand leader of that time, Lokmanya Tilak, favoured 'Poorna Swaraj', full and instant freedom. There were other leaders who gave their lives for the freedom struggle and were respected by both groups. Gokhale was a moderate. Lokmanya Tilak a radical. Gandhi aligned with Gokhale.

The unruly behaviour that is common to parliamentary and legislative proceedings today was foreshadowed at the Surat session of the Congress in December 1907. The moderates Pherozeshah Mehta and Surendranath Banerjea were on the dais. Chappals were thrown at them. Turbans were snatched, chairs were broken. Humiliatingly, British police had to come in and restore order. This incident was at the back of Gandhi's mind. Among the radicals, besides Tilak, were Aurobindo Ghose, Lala Lajpat Rai and Bipin Chandra Pal.

Savarkar's entire book is a eulogy to ancient India. When one is so immersed in the act of praising something, one loses oneself in it. In such a state, everything of the past appears glorious. But if you read an epic like Vyasa's Mahabharata, you find all the ills that plague modern society in it: desire, deception, lust, blasphemy, cruelty, jealousy and violence towards animals. Vedavyasa the poet saint was a visionary. He declares, 'No matter how vehemently I denounced immorality, nobody seems to have heeded my voice.' This is significant.

After showing Arjuna the 'vishwaroopa',[2] Krishna advises him to exert his own will. Yet Arjuna, in spite of experiencing this vision, continues to make the same mistakes. In the Ramayana, when Hanuman goes to Lanka in search of Sita, he walks straight into Ravana's harem. He finds several women passionately embracing each other. Chhi, he exclaims, dismayed that he was looking for a chaste woman like Sita in such a place.

Just as our great epics are testimony to a glorious past, they are also a record of our base behaviour.

It is believed that each time the world degenerated, one of the dashavatars, the ten incarnations, cleansed it. This is our story. Savarkar uses the past to motivate us towards nation building. Like Muhammad Ali Jinnah, he was a rationalist who did not believe in religion. That is why he does not formulate his idea of Hindutva through the Hindu religion. Like Gandhi and Ambedkar, he opposes untouchability. He wants a strong India based on Hindutva. For him, not everybody who lives in Hindustan is a Hindu. Only those who embrace India as their punyabhoomi form the core of this country, he says. People from different countries live in America. When World War I broke out, though, did the Germans not swear allegiance to Germany, Savarkar asks.

9

In a little state with a small population, I would
    so order it,
that, though there were individuals with the
    abilities of ten or a
hundred men, there should be no employment
    of them; I would make the
people, while looking on death as a grievous
    thing, yet not remove
elsewhere (to avoid it).

Though they had boats and carriages, they
    should have no occasion
to ride in them; though they had buff coats and
    sharp weapons, they
should have no occasion to don or use them.

I would make the people return to the use of
    knotted cords (instead of written characters).

They should think their (coarse) food sweet;
    their (plain) clothes
beautiful; their (poor) dwellings places of rest;
    and their common
ways sources of enjoyment.

There should be a neighbouring state within
    sight, and the voices
of the fowls and dogs should be heard all the way
    from it to us, but I
would make the people to old age, even to death,
    not have any
intercourse with it.

                              (Poem 80, Tao Te Ching)[1]

A foreigner went to Ramana Maharshi and said,
'I have come to be converted to Hinduism. This
is my punyabhoomi.'

Ramana Maharshi replied, 'Is it right to say
that, in the whole world, all of which is God's
creation, there are only some punyabhoomis?'

One of his disciples told me this story. For
Ramana, the Arunachala mountain where he
dwelt was his punyabhoomi. There was blistering
hot sun there. If he sat under a tree, there were
swarms of honeybees that would sting him. The
undulating land with its ups and downs would

exhaust him. The place was also a hideout where he could stretch his tired limbs on smooth, well-worn rocks. Ramana, who loved all animals, built a tomb for the crow who used to sit on the well in his backyard. When he was dying of cancer, the peacocks he used to feed began to screech for food. Even as he took his last breath, Ramana told his disciples to feed the birds, as he would on any other day.

Kashi is a punyabhoomi for all. When Gandhi returned from Africa and went there on a pilgrimage, he found it unbearably filthy. How is it possible to call this a punyabhoomi, he asks. He sets up his ashram in the sweltering hot town of Wardha. In 1940, when St Paul's Cathedral in London was bombed, Gandhi writes that he felt as if the bomb had fallen on Kashi. Thus the concept of punyabhoomi is not confined to one country, it could be any place. While Savarkar the rationalist fervently praises the supporters of Hindutva, the religious Gandhi offers a liberating text to all humanity in his *Hind Swaraj*.

Savarkar's ideology is based, in essence, on the concept of Hindus who share 'blood ties' and acknowledge India as punyabhoomi. As opposed to this, Gandhi through his conversation in *Hind Swaraj* presents two different perspectives of a modern concept of civilization that would appeal to Indians. People like Naoroji and Gokhale were dear to him. While he respects the eminence of Tilak, he has a fondness for the moderate Gokhale.

During one of the huge satyagrahas Gandhi had called for, an Englishman was killed because of the mean-mindedness of the people. He called off the satyagraha, although his followers felt that withdrawing a rapidly growing struggle was not right. Gandhi calls his failure to recognize that there were still some people who were not ready for a non-violent struggle 'a Himalayan blunder'.

In another essay, 'The India of My Dreams', Gandhi writes that no army can vanquish India, which is made up of innumerable small, independent, self-ruled villages. This porcupine-like India, even with a small army, will remain unconquerable.

In this way, two visions of India emerge at the beginning of the twentieth century. One was an all-inclusive India that was local and decentralized in the form of panchayats. The other emotionally charged vision denied its multilingual, multi-religious nature and was limited to those who considered it their punyabhoomi. Hitler did the same in Germany. The whites in Germany were deemed Aryans. The Jews, non-Aryans. The Jews were sent to concentration camps and exterminated. The Germans made rings and bangles from their charred bones. Even as the Jews were being exterminated, Germany widened its roads. Industries that fed the war flourished. People exulted in the arrogance of their superiority.

In the time and the context in which it was written, Savarkar's argument was not as extreme as Hitler's, but it had all the potential to incite cruelty. Inspired by him, people were willing to sacrifice their lives. Nathuram Godse was one of them. That the Congress was capable of the same sort of brutality was evident in the massacre of Sikhs after Indira Gandhi's assassination.

It is a mindset. Gandhi's life was a rejection of that mindset. Even his end refuted it. In the neo-nationalist discourse that prevails today, people believe that it is possible to cultivate this mindset without any associated guilt. The Muslims of India light the fire of resistance only to get burnt themselves. The seeds of hatred which Gandhi's Noakhali yatra could not suppress continue to grow as trees of death in Pakistan with encouragement from its military.

While Savarkar's writing stems from a heightened emotional state, Gandhi's passes through the sieve of introspection.

Deliberation is not a characteristic of modern civilization. The visual media thinks in a rush of relentlessly moving images. It is quite natural then for present-day Savarkarites to think that Gandhi's writing, which looked for the violence within to reject it, amounted to timidity. But Gandhi asks himself some tough questions.

Why are the British here?

Because we too love modern civilization.

Why should we oppose modern civilization?

To liberate not only the Indians but the British as well.

The fact that he wrote *Hind Swaraj*, which makes this argument in his mother tongue Gujarati, is important.

Nehru is critical of *Hind Swaraj*. In a letter that Gandhi writes to this dear disciple of his in 1945, here is what he says: 'You are going to be the leader of independent India. But you don't seem to have read my *Hind Swaraj*.' Nehru's affectionate and respectful reply was, 'I read it long ago. I do not agree with your views. India's villages are hellholes of superstition.' (Ambedkar also believed that Indian villages were hell.)

The term 'modern civilization' was used sarcastically by Gandhi. When he visited Britain for the Round Table Conference, a journalist asked him, 'What do you think of modern civilization?' Gandhi replied, 'It is a good idea.'

Gandhi was not one to regret the past. His vision of Sarvodaya,[2] more relevant today than ever, included every individual – no matter where he lived and thrived and flourished. He believed that it was possible for a person to instantly change into this ideal citizen. Such a citizen will also evolve continuously throughout his lifetime.

Gandhiji asked only his ashramites to follow the code of the ashram in their daily lives. There was always coffee for Rajaji and cigarettes for Azad and Nehru when they went there for meetings. He did not succeed in ridding Kasturba of her coffee addiction. (I for one would not willingly live in Gandhi's ashram.)

In this context, I am reminded of Tagore's *Gora*, a canonical text. The hero of the novel subscribes to an extreme form of Hinduism. He clings to his faith and denounces the Brahmo Samaj, which has a flavour of Christianity, a love for the English language and an arrogance in its superiority. The light-skinned Gora was not aware that he was born in a stable to an Irish couple who were fleeing from the rioters during the Sepoy Mutiny, and the woman he loved and looked up to was his foster-mother. His foster-father was a selfish man and a sanatani, an orthodox and ritualistic Hindu. To hide the fact that Gora was not his son, he even performed the boy's thread ceremony. And yet, when he was performing a puja at home, he would not touch Gora. Later, Gora – brought up as a staunch Hindu – discovers that he is an outsider. He adopts his mother's humanism as his religion and becomes a Vishwamanava (Universal Man). Transcending the inhibitions of a sanatani and the anglicized cosmopolitanism of the Brahmo Samaj, he becomes an Indian.

When the Babri Masjid was demolished by the Hindutvavadis, I was the president of the Sahitya Akademi in Delhi. I tried to encourage everybody across the country to discuss *Gora*. This work is critical to my study of Hindutva. I urge the readers, to study *Gora* in order to understand my brief thoughts on it.

What has emerged from our study so far is this: It is not cowardice that counters Savarkar's egocentric aggressive standpoint or Gora's sanatani faith. It is selfless compassion. It is the path of the Buddha who in his time took shelter under the Kshatriyas.

In our times, Gandhi followed the path of egoless fearlessness. He respected the moderates but was extreme in his own way.

Even today, there are many people who practise a Hindutva that is not articulated clearly even to themselves. Among them are both upper-caste and lower-caste Hindus and those who fit Savarkar's definition of Hindutvavadi. In their view, the cosmopolitan Congress leaders appear as escapists who not only cannot stand up to the Muslims but also pander to them for their votes. In this situation, it seems like only Modi has the kshatra quality to rule this country with chaturopaya,[3] by silencing the Muslims of this country and appeasing the avaricious ones among them. They don't see this trait in the well-mannered Advani who inadvertently praised Jinnah. The person who seemed to rival Modi for a brief while was Arvind Kejriwal, who did not hesitate to be seen as a practising Hindu and posed for cameras with his bare, vibhuti-smeared body after a dip in the Ganga. In these elections, Kejriwal alone countered Modi's Hindutva intellectually as well as through simple Hindu rituals. Rahul Gandhi, with his liberal European mindset and a half-baked cosmopolitanism, speaking some Hindi but better English could not weather the storm of Hindutva. The low-caste leader from Gujarat became the ideal, like Shivaji, for Indians who had a deep-seated longing for kshatra qualities. He rekindled memories of Vivekananda.

It was possible, in ancient India, for a low-caste individual to become a ruler. A Shudra with his bravery could climb the caste ladder and become a Kshatriya. Shivaji was crowned like this. I believe that this egalitarian dream, so dear to many of us, is realized today in Modi – not because of the Sangh Parivar's ideology, but because of the environment created by Gandhi, Ambedkar and V.P. Singh. This environment became necessary for the Sangh Parivar as well.

When I was in Kerala, I invited V.P. Singh to our university. At breakfast I asked him, 'When you were in the Congress for so long, you did not think about the upliftment of the "Mandal" castes. What you are doing now, is it political?'

After thinking for a moment, he replied, 'It is not only *my* politics. All political parties will have to bring it into practice.'

I recalled what he had said sometime later. On the occasion of the Padma Awards ceremony, the friendly Advaniji came up to Esther and me at teatime and spoke to her in Kannada, saying, 'Hegde taught me this in jail.' After some polite conversation, he said to me, 'See how times have changed. All these days, I looked upon Kalyan Singh only as a party colleague. Today I am compelled to notice his caste.'

If Kejriwal took a dip in the Ganga, Modi performed an arti to the river. After Modi won the elections, a joyous Indian media projected amplified images of his calm, contented, smiling face. Over and over, they showed Modi offering flowers and paying his respects before a small photograph of Gandhi. Gradually, the Gujarat riots grew into a myth, like the one of Arjuna setting fire to the Khandava forest, a symbol of his bravery. It is a sign of the new times that Gopal Subramaniam, who reminds one of past events, was prevented from being appointed a Supreme Court judge. Subramanian Swamy justified this by saying that the stand Gopal Subramaniam took during the Ram Setu controversy was not right. Though Subramaniam was a very senior advocate, he did not subscribe to the ideology on which the elections were won.

Let us go back to *Hind Swaraj*, a work contemporary of, and an alternative to,

Savarkar's *Hindutva*. In this book, Gandhi's clarity of thought comes from the greatness of ancient India as well as the meanness of its decadent practices. In his words, Gandhi paid more attention to the greatness, but in his actions, he focused on its meanness. Like untouchability, casteism and unclean holy places that discriminated among people on the basis of their caste. Gandhi observed a fast for one day because Kasturba, along with his secretary Desai, went to the Puri Jagannath temple where untouchables were not allowed. This is how he acted. Gandhi's egoless courage is unique in that it allows him to reject modern medicine, the British Parliament, railways, lawyers and doctors. Some of his words are as follows:

> Nothing can equal seeds sown by ancestors, Rome went, Greece shared the same fate, the might of the Pharaohs was broken, Japan has become Westernized, of China nothing can be said. But India is still somehow or other, sound at the foundation.
>
> Civilization is that mode of conduct which points out to man the path of duty.

> Performance of duty and observance of morality are convertible terms. To observe morality is to attain mastery over our mind and our passions. So doing, we know ourselves. The Gujarati equivalent for civilization means good conduct.[4]

If Savarkarism is a display of valour, Gandhism advocates morality and self-realization. Even as he builds the argument, Gandhi recalls the Gujarati word for 'civilization'. His modernism is not cosmopolitan. It has its roots in Gujarati, it grew in India and its branches spread across the sky. In the early twentieth century, these two Indias, the cosmopolitan and the other rooted in India, germinated among the Indians living in England, and sprouted and spread to India as well.

Gandhi respected Tilak but chose Gokhale as his guru. For the radicals of that time, Gokhale was a coward.

An exploration of various texts has revealed that my view that the Hindutva of bravery and a universal religiosity that supports lower communities are two separate entities is superficial. In the Congress, the views of those who did not subscribe fully to Gandhi's ideology had an element of aggression in them, even if they were not as extreme as Savarkar's.

Once Masti,[5] whom I revered, came to attend my talk on Gandhi. After everyone had left, he called me to his side and said warmly, 'No doubt Gandhi was a Purushottama. A Mahatma. But he did not pay attention to kshatra dharma.' These words of Masti have remained with me, without acceptance or opposition.

Among Gandhi's followers were both devout but liberal Muslims like Maulana Azad and militant Hindus. Those freedom fighters who eventually succeeded in the Congress in the Nehruvian era were the cosmopolites with a vision of British socialism and eager for development. The leftists wanted India to develop an atom bomb. Mao's China, which encroached on our territory, attacked and overpowered us, also announced its atom bomb. A few years later, the India of Gandhi's satyagraha tested its atom bomb. Marxism has a way of accepting certain unavoidable realities as tactics. If Gandhi, who believed that human beings were capable of instant change in their personal lives, their thoughts and their behaviour, had lived for ten years more, he would have been a daily embarrassment for the government. While

Godse caused the government to feel orphaned, he saved it from embarrassment. That is the harsh truth.

Lohia refers to Nehru as a cosmopolite and Gandhi a universalist. He illustrates this through an incident. When Lohia and Nehru were still friends, they went for a walk in a wide open space. Pointing to this expanse, Nehru is supposed to have said, 'You and I come from this kind of land. We have universal vision. Gandhiji is a saint, but coming from a small province, he cannot grasp the world in its vastness.' Lohia admitted regretfully that he had agreed with it at that time. In the Lohia I admired, I saw the desire for kshatra as well as Gandhi's anarchy, which came from a belief in total decentralization. Gandhi's anarchy, like Tolstoy's, defies all authority, and can sprout anywhere, like a blade of grass does. Tolstoy lies buried under a simple grassy mound. Lohia, who knew these philosophies intimately, still had a longing for kshatra. He once advised the liberal-minded: 'India has not experienced statehood. And even if it has, it was a long time ago. After that it was ruled by the Mughals and the British. Russia and China, which underwent an intellectual revolution, had a cruel system. But it was their own rule, not one imposed by a foreign power. That's why today to deny the desire for Indian statehood would be an act of cowardice.' It is not surprising that the Lohia who said these words would take this insistent stance: 'Nehru should immediately withdraw Section 370 that is applicable to Kashmir.' He argued for a common law for Muslims and Hindus. Kishen Pattanayak, who argued similarly, lost the election. To Lohia, saying things that people did not like and consequently losing the election were just one phase of the dharma of politics. In the end, he had advised his followers to be prepared to do their duty despite disappointment and keep alive the dream of socialism that would be realized in a hundred years.

Another example of Lohia's youthful zeal is his idea of an undivided India. He would say, if necessary, let the prime minister of Pakistan become the president of the Union. When China attacked India, he felt that Nehru could have asked Kennedy for an atom bomb. When he was once visiting Mysore, Lohia invited me to the Brindavan Hotel where he was staying, for breakfast and gave me a piece of affectionate advice: 'Use Kannada for undergraduate studies in Karnataka. After that, for postgraduate courses, let Hindi be the medium.'

Instantly, I told the genial Lohia, 'If a language does not deserve to be a medium at the postgraduate level, it is also unworthy for the primary level.'

Lohia accepted my view without hesitation. 'True. In that case, let India be a multilingual nation. In Parliament, let all Indian languages be used with translations as is done in the United Nations.'

It was Lohia who made it possible for J.H. Patel to speak in Kannada in Parliament.

I suspect that he never got over the idea of a strong nation. But his strong nation was not the holy land of Hindus. He dreamt of a time when it would be possible to travel the world without a passport.

Lohia did not live to see the Emergency. His desire for all non-Congress parties to come together was fulfilled under the leadership of Jayaprakash Narayan. At that time, my friend Madhwarao, a leader of the Rashtriya Swayamsevak Sangh's intellectual circle, came to my small house in Mysore, riding pillion on somebody's scooter. I was surprised to see him transformed. He was usually dressed in the Sangh Parivar uniform, but that day he came wearing a T-shirt and trousers.

As he settled down, Madhwarao said, 'You must be surprised at my clothes. I have gone underground now.'

I asked him a question then. 'Why do you oppose Indira Gandhi? I just don't understand it. She dismissed the DMK government that was inimical to the Aryans. She enforced family planning programmes on Muslims to prevent them from having too many children. She split Pakistan and facilitated the creation of Bangladesh. She got India the atom bomb. By annexing Sikkim, she expanded the country. She made sure trains ran on time. The idea of Savarkar's India was reinforced through Indira Gandhi. Why then do you oppose her?'

An intellectual like Madhwarao had no answer to this. A few years later, when Vajpayee, whom Govindacharya described as 'just a mask', was the prime minister, some prominent RSS leaders said that Indira Gandhi was our true leader.

Allow me to offer a clarification here. No Congress government has ever accepted Hindutva or Savarkar's concept of punyabhoomi. Lohia himself was not at all influenced by this idea. Gandhi and Tagore held that even a broad-minded idea of nationalism is dangerous. But none of the Congress leaders shared this view.

We continued to govern in a manner in which the desire for Hindutva could be aroused. We became friends with Israel. (There is a possibility that, under Modi's leadership, we could become like Israel.)

Gandhi alone in independent India foresaw this danger. Gandhi marched in Noakhali barefoot, put his celibacy to test, suffered great pain internally and externally, saved the lives of Hindus and came to Delhi on his way to Punjab. He noticed that Vallabhbhai Patel, who had come to receive him at the railway station, was not his usual self. Seeing the normally humorous and cheerful Patel so dejected, Gandhi asked with paternal concern what had come over him. Delhi is no longer the Delhi of old. The radical nationalist Hindutvavadis have taken over all the mosques of Delhi. Thousands of fearful Muslims have abandoned their homes and fled to Karachi. Deeply disturbed by this, Gandhi angrily ordered Patel, the then home minister, to immediately remove the Hindus who were occupying the mosques. He urged Patel to bring back the Muslims who had fled to Karachi and reinstate them in their homes.

This was in January 1948. People who were close to Gandhi reported that they heard him talking to himself. They said Gandhi sometimes considered himself a Pakistani just as he considered himself a Hindustani. He was grieved that Islam was being destroyed in India and in Pakistan. Without consulting anyone, he started an indefinite fast. His health deteriorated. The fast made him weak and frail. I remember reading somewhere that the RSS, the Jamat-e-Islam and Sir Muhammad Zafarullah Khan, an Ahmadiya Muslim from Pakistan, all pleaded with him to give up his fast. Gandhi is supposed to have asked the then Governor General, Sir Mountbatten, 'Can we refuse to pay the Rs 55 crore India had agreed to give Pakistan because they moved their army into Kashmir?' Mountbatten had replied that it was only fair to pay it. I learnt this from an article written by Vinay Lal. By not taking even his beloved Nehru and Patel into confidence, Gandhi isolated himself as he embarked on that fast. There were many who wished for his death. But Gandhi's fast was primarily to question, on moral grounds, because he opposed kshatra, the nationalism that was taking root in India. Nehru and Patel were statists.[6] The prevailing atmosphere in the country was to resist pressure from the Muslims and stand firm.

Gandhi did not lose. But neither did Savarkar. On Gandhi's insistence, Rs 55 crore were paid to Pakistan. It infuriated the people. But popularity did not matter to Gandhi. Truth did. He showed the world that it is important for a strong government to observe a code of ethics. No country will observe such a code if it conflicts with their interests of power. They will succumb only to pressure. What we need to remember is that in our independent India, neither Savarkar lost nor Gandhi. Some intellectuals amongst us objected to India going nuclear. But people who leaned to the right lauded the 'smiling Buddha'.

After Modi came to power, it would appear that all leftist ideas have been decimated. One of the reasons for this is that, gradually, mouthing leftist ideas has become easy. As for secularism, it was little more than a convenient term. Yet, because India is a democracy, the right to information and schemes like the midday meal in schools have kept our self-respect intact.

On leftist words becoming mere sounds, Gopalakrishna Adiga has written a humorous poem. It begins like this: 'Leaning to the left, flashing their left eyebrow, they are coming, they are coming, the land surveyors are coming.' Now changing it slightly, we can say, 'Leaning to the right, flashing their right eyebrow, they are coming, they are coming, the brazen crooks are coming.' For whether it is the highly eloquent English media or the Hindi media, they are learning a new language, one that is acceptable to Modi.

On Gandhi's death, the Kannada poet V. Seetharamaiah made a significant statement. 'All of us are like the serpent, full of poison. Godse is only its fangs.'

10

Nathuram Godse's last speech is worthy of attention. During his trial, Gandhi's assassin read out from typewritten pages a statement in court on why he killed Gandhi. His thesis was ninety pages long. For five hours, he stood and spoke. It was like a mirror held up to his inner life; it has also become a statement to illustrate the influence that Gandhi could have had on India. That statement reveals both Godse, who viewed Gandhi as an enemy, and Gandhi.

Godse was born in a religious Brahmin family. Because of this, he says, he grew up with a love for the Hindu religion, Hindu history and Hindu culture. The following is an excerpt from his speech:[1]

> As I grew up I developed a tendency to free
> thinking unfettered by any superstitious

allegiance to any 'isms', political or religious. That is why I worked actively for the eradication of untouchability and the caste system based on birth alone. I openly joined anti-caste movements and maintained that all Hindus are of equal status as to rights, social and religious, and should be considered high or low on merit alone and not through the accident of birth in a particular caste or profession.

I used publicly to take part in organized anti-caste dinners in which thousands of Hindus, Brahmins, Vaishyas, Kshatriyas, Chamars and Bhangis participated. We broke the caste rules and dined in the company of each other. I have read the speeches and writings of Dadabhai Naoroji, Vivekananda, Gokhale, Tilak, along with the books of ancient and modern history of India and some prominent countries like England, France, America and Russia. Moreover, I studied the tenets of Socialism and Marxism. But above all I studied very closely what Veer Savarkar and Gandhiji had written and spoken, as, to my mind, these two ideologies have contributed more to the moulding of the thought and action of the Indian people during the last thirty years or so than any other factor has done.

All this thinking and reading led me to believe that it was my first duty to serve Hindudom and Hindus both as a patriot and as a world citizen. To secure the freedom and to safeguard the just interests of some thirty crore Hindus would automatically constitute the freedom and well-being of all India, one-fifth of the human race.

Since the year 1920, that is, after the demise of Lokmanya Tilak, Gandhi's influence in the Congress first increased and then became supreme.

His activities for public awakening were phenomenal in their intensity and were reinforced by the slogan of truth and non-violence, which he paraded ostentatiously before the country. No sensible or enlightened person could object to these slogans. In fact, there is nothing new or original in them. They are implicit in every constitutional public movement. But it is nothing but a dream if you imagine the bulk of mankind is, or can ever become, capable of scrupulous adherence to these lofty principles in its normal life from day to day. In fact, honour, duty and love of one's own kith and kin and country might often compel us to disregard non-violence and to use force. I could never conceive that an armed resistance to an aggression is unjust.

I would consider it a religious and moral duty to resist and if possible, to overpower such an enemy by use of force. In the Ramayana Rama killed Ravana in a tumultuous fight and relieved Sita. [In the Mahabharata] Krishna killed Kansa to end his wickedness; and Arjuna had to fight and slay quite a number of his friends and relations, including the revered Bhishma, because the latter was on the side of the aggressor. It is my firm belief that in dubbing Rama, Krishna and Arjuna as guilty of violence, the Mahatma betrayed a total ignorance of the springs of human action. In more recent history, it was the heroic fight put up by Chhatrapati Shivaji that first checked and eventually destroyed Muslim tyranny in India. It was absolutely essential for Shivaji to overpower and kill an aggressive Afzal Khan, failing which he would have lost his own life. In condemning history's towering warriors like Shivaji, Rana Pratap and Guru Gobind Singh as misguided patriots, Gandhi has merely exposed his self-conceit.

He was, paradoxical as it may appear, a violent pacifist who brought untold calamities on the country in the name of truth and non-violence, while Rana Pratap, Shivaji and the Guru will remain enshrined in the hearts of their countrymen forever for the freedom they brought to them. The accumulating provocation of thirty-two years, culminating in his last pro-Muslim fast, at last goaded me to the conclusion that the existence of Gandhi should be brought to an end immediately. Gandhi had done very good work in South Africa to uphold the rights and well-being of the Indian community there.

But when he finally returned to India, he developed a subjective mentality under which he alone was to be the final judge of what was right or wrong. If the country wanted his leadership, it had to accept his infallibility; if it did not, he would stand aloof from the Congress and carry on in his own way. Against such an attitude there can be no halfway house. Either Congress had to surrender its will to his and be content with playing second fiddle to all his eccentricity, whimsicality, metaphysics and primitive vision, or it had to carry on without him. He alone was the judge of everyone and everything; he was the master brain guiding the Civil Disobedience Movement; no other could know the technique of that movement. He alone knew when to begin it and when to withdraw it. The movement might succeed or fail, but that could make no difference to the Mahatma's infallibility. 'A Satyagrahi can never fail' was his formula for his own infallibility, and nobody except himself knew what a Satyagrahi is. Thus the Mahatma became the judge and the jury in his own case. [...]

In the beginning of his career in India, Gandhi gave a great impetus to Hindi, but as he found that the Muslims did not like it, he became a champion of what is called Hindustani. Everybody in India knows that there is no language in India called Hindustani; it has no grammar; it has no vocabulary. It is a mere dialect; it is spoken, not written. It is a tongue and a cross-breed between Hindi and Urdu, and not even the Mahatma's sophistry could make it popular. But in his desire to please the Muslims he insisted that Hindustani alone should be the national language of India. [...]

From August 1946 onwards, the private armies of the Muslim League began a massacre of Hindus. The then Viceroy, Lord Wavell, though distressed at what was happening, would not use his powers under the Government of India Act of 1935 to prevent the rape, murder and arson. Hindu blood began to flow from Bengal to Karachi with little retaliation by the Hindus. [...]

Lord Wavell had to resign as he could not bring about a settlement and was succeeded by Lord Mountbatten. [...]

The Congress, which had boasted of its nationalism and socialism, secretly accepted Pakistan literally at the point of the bayonet and abjectly surrendered to Jinnah. India was vivisected and one-third of the Indian territory became foreign land to us from 15 August 1947. Lord Mountbatten came to be described in the Congress circles as the greatest Viceroy and Governor-General this country ever had. [...]

The Hindu-Muslim unity bubble was finally burst and a theocratic state was established with the consent of Nehru and his crowd and they have called it 'freedom won by them with sacrifice' – whose sacrifice? When top leaders of Congress, with the consent of Gandhi, divided and tore the country – which we considered a deity of worship – my mind was filled with direful anger.

What Godse says here is not true. Gandhi opposed Partition till the end. He tried a different approach. Or you could call it a tactic. He called Mountbatten and told him, 'Go now. Don't divide the nation. Let us allay the fears of Jinnah that the Hindus will not do justice by the Muslims by making him the prime minister of our independent nation. We will continue our dialogue with him.' Baffled by this, Mountbatten mentioned it to Nehru and Patel. Then Nehru and Patel went up to Gandhi and told him that the time was now past; nothing could be done. His words would have no effect on India, and rivers of blood would flow. With this they frightened him. Gandhi fell silent. On the day of India's Independence, he went to Bengal to prevent the communal violence and killings there. He saved several lives. Muslims surrendered their weapons at Gandhi's feet. He made it possible by walking barefoot through filth and broken glass. This is the most significant achievement of his entire life. But Godse didn't see this. To a mind possessed by Savarkar's idea of Hindutva, these truths were invisible.

And so let's return to Godse's speech.[2]

One of the conditions imposed by Gandhi for his breaking of the fast related to the mosques in Delhi occupied by the Hindu refugees. But when Hindus in Pakistan were subjected to violent attacks, he did not so much as utter a single word to protest and censure the Pakistan government or the Muslims concerned. Gandhi was shrewd enough to know that while undertaking a fast unto death, had he imposed some conditions on the Muslims in Pakistan, there would have been found hardly any Muslims who could have shown some grief if the fast had ended in his death. It was for this reason that he purposely avoided imposing any conditions on the Muslims.

He was fully aware from past experience that Jinnah was not at all perturbed or influenced by his fast and the Muslim League hardly attached any value to the inner voice of Gandhi. Gandhi is being referred to as the Father of the Nation. But if that is so, he has failed in his paternal duty in as much he has acted treacherously to the nation by his consenting to the partitioning of it. I stoutly maintain that Gandhi has failed in his duty. He has proved to be the Father of Pakistan. His inner voice, his spiritual power, his doctrine of non-violence of which so much is made, all crumbled against Jinnah's iron will and proved to be powerless.

Briefly speaking, I thought to myself and foresaw that I shall be totally ruined, and the only thing I could expect from the people would be nothing but hatred and that I shall have lost all my honour, even more valuable than my life, if I were to kill Gandhiji. But at the same time, I thought that the Indian politics in the absence of Gandhiji would surely be practical, able to retaliate and would be powerful with the armed forces. No doubt, my own future would be totally ruined, but the nation would be saved from the inroads of Pakistan. People may even call me or dub me as devoid of any sense or foolish, but the nation would be free to follow the course founded on reason, which I consider necessary for sound nation-building.

After having fully considered the question, I took the final decision in the matter, but I did not speak about it to anyone whatsoever. I took courage in both my hands and I did fire the shots at Gandhiji on 30th January 1948, on the prayer grounds in Birla House. I do say that my shots were fired at the person whose policy and action had brought rack and ruin and destruction to millions of Hindus. There was no legal machinery by which such an offender could be brought to book and for this reason I fired those fatal shots. I bear no ill will towards anyone individually, but I do say that I had no respect for the present government owing to their policy, which was unfairly favourable towards the Muslims. But at the same time I could clearly see that the policy was entirely due to the presence of Gandhi.

I have to say with great regret that Prime Minister Nehru quite forgets that his preaching and deeds are at times at variance with each other when he talks about India as a secular state in season and out of season, because it is significant to note that Nehru has played a leading role in the theocratic state of Pakistan, and his job was made easier by Gandhi's persistent policy of appeasement towards the Muslims. I now stand before the court to accept the full share of my responsibility for what I have done and the judge would, of course, pass against me such orders of sentence as may be considered proper. But I would like to add that I do not desire any mercy to be shown to me, nor do I wish that anyone should beg for mercy on my behalf.

My confidence about the moral side of my action has not been shaken even by the criticism levelled against it on all sides. I have no doubt that honest writers of history will weigh my act and find the true value thereof someday in future.

This is the sum of what Godse has said. There is clarity in his vision. There is an awareness that he is killing a man of Gandhi's stature. His position is that the country comes before a great saint. It is Savarkar's writings that have made such a thought process possible. His ideology makes it possible to only contemplate that which is relevant from India's glorious past and forget about the contributions made by people of diverse faiths and castes in modern times. Not only that, this approach encourages even the slightest prejudice that any Indian might have against the Muslims. Surreptitiously. Even when you join your hands before Gandhi.

Epilogue

• Whether it is Godse or Savarkar, what they broadly wanted was unity of the Hindus of India. A unity that ignores the inherent diversity, and silences those who do not consider India their punyabhoomi. Without this unity it is impossible to build a strong nation. Some Muslims in Pakistan also think along these lines. But Bangladesh separated primarily because of language. Blood was shed.

• The unity that Gandhi desired was one in which everyone retained their faith, preserved their own unique cultures and accepted ahimsa. Unity comes naturally to those who live in harmony despite their differences. This becomes possible when ahimsa is the basis of their lives. The life force of every community lies in its uniqueness. Whether it is food, games, worship, dress, concept of God, differing methods of prayer, the many climates that nurture mountains, forests, valleys, flora and fauna – they are all part of a chain. This multiplicity is the warp and weft of the ecological system of the living world. In a desert, Allah is God. The only God for the Muslims. For the Hindus who live in diverse climates, God assumes different qualities. In central India, he becomes Krishna of the Krishna Leela. For the Bengali writer Bankim Chandra Chattopadhyay, there are two Krishnas. One was the Radharamana of the Leela, dear to poets. And the other was Krishna of the Mahabharata, a shrewd politician feared by the enemy. We needed the second Krishna to align with the British and defeat the Muslims. And later we needed him to defeat the British themselves. In north India, God becomes Maryada Purushottama[1] Rama. In south India and Kashmir, he becomes Shiva. Allah who had to live here got acclimatized too. Muslim and Christian conversion programmes did not work as well in India as they did in other lands. Because for the ordinary people, especially in the rural areas, the Muslims were just another caste worshipping a different God. Like all the other castes, they were also one of us. In the village where I grew up, when children fell ill, people usually made a vow to Allah.

• Gandhi considered himself also a Muslim. The Sufi saints who were born in Persia and flourished in India are respected by both Hindus and Muslims. Although, of course, orthodox Muslims do not accept them because the Sufis believe in one God and perceive Him as Ram–Rahim.

• My favourite definition of Unity in Diversity is this: If we take unity to an extreme and seek to destroy diversity (as Savarkar did), diversity becomes important. If you keep diversity as the centre and take it to an extreme, you get the feeling that India is one. Our differences do not seem so significant.

• The ideas of Savarkar's India and Gandhi's decentralized India that belonged to everybody did not remain very different after Independence. What the Sangh Parivar could not do, Indira Gandhi did. During his regime, Atal Bihari Vajpayee brought India and Pakistan a little closer. He ruled as a tall leader reminiscent of Nehru.

• Now Modi, advocate of Hindu unity, with no regret for the Muslims massacred in Gujarat which he had ruled unopposed, has set out to make a strong India ruled by the corporates.

• What we need at the moment is not development. We need Sarvodaya. Had Gandhi lived, he would have recommended Sarvodaya to a world that is gasping because of modern development.

There is one hope. It is true that Lohia's principles for the upliftment of Shudras ended up becoming Yadavized. And Ambedkar's principles became Mayawati's statues. The communists in Bengal have now lost their ground. In Modi's enthusiasm for development, the atmosphere is further filled with factory smoke. Tribals who live close to nature have nowhere to go. In the hubris of extreme progress, man, suffering revulsion from excessive consumption, may see the need for change.

If not, the Earth will speak.

Notes

Chapter 1

1   Satvik: Analytical, sober, gentle.

2   Rajasik: Action-oriented, more reactive, less analytical.

3   Kshatra/kshatra dharma: Implies temporal authority and power, which was based less on being a successful leader in battle and more on the tangible power of laying claim to sovereignty over a territory, and symbolizing ownership over clan lands. This later gave rise to the idea of kingship.

4   IT–BT: Information technology and biotechnology.

5   Dattatreya: Considered an incarnation of Brahma, Vishnu and Shiva, Dattatreya is always accompanied by four dogs of four colours.

6   Mahasammata: Literally, the Great Elect. According to Buddhist tradition, he was the first monarch of the world.

7   Akshaya patra: A magical vessel that can provide a never-ending supply of food. Surya, the sun god, gave it to Yudhishthira so that the Pandavas had food every day.

Chapter 2

1   The Khandava forest: The Mahabharata speaks of it as inhabited by serpents. Krishna and Arjuna cleared the forest by setting fire to it, killing the inhabitants of the forest.

2   Parikshit: The grandson of Arjuna and Subhadra, and the son of Abhimanyu and his wife Uttara.

Chapter 3

1   Murari: After Krishna destroyed the fortified city of Pragjyotisha, slew Mura, a great demon, and burnt his 7,000 sons, he came to be known as Murari. (The word 'ari' means enemy.)

Chapter 4

1   http://www.sacred-texts.com/tao/taote.htm

2   Ras Kreeda: The dance of Krishna with the gopis of Brindavan, where he danced with every single one of them simultaneously. It symbolizes the relationship between the finite soul (jiva) and the Supreme self (Paramatma).

3   Raj dharma: The duty of the rulers, which was intrinsically entwined with the concept of bravery and Kshatra dharma.

Chapter 6

1   http://www.savarkar.org/content/pdfs/en/essentials_of_hindutva.v001.pdf, p. 3, accessed 15 January 2016.

2 Varnashrama dharma: Duties performed according to the system of four varnas (social divisions) and four ashramas (stages in life).

3 Sanatani: A term that is used to describe those who practise Sanatana dharma (Hinduism). The term was popularized by Mahatma Gandhi in 1921.

4 Panchama: The lowest caste groups in India.

5 Samartha Ramdas: A noted seventeenth-century saint and spiritual poet of Maharashtra and guru to Chhatrapati Shivaji. He is most remembered for his Advaita Vendatist text, the *Dasbodh*.

6 Kavi Bhushan: A poet in the courts of the Bundeli king Chhatrasal and the Maratha king Shivaji. He mainly wrote in Brajbhasha interspersed with words from Sanskrit, Arabic and Persian.

7 *Shiva Shivah na Hindu na Yavanah*: Shiva is Shiva, neither a Hindu nor a yavana (a foreigner).

8 Pratisarga Parva: The genealogy of kings and sages. It is written as a universal history.

9 *Bhavishya Purana*: One of the eighteen major Hindu Puranas, it is attributed to Vyasa, the compiler of the Vedas. The *Bhavishya Purana*, as the name suggests, contains prophecies regarding the future.

10 http://www.savarkar.org/content/pdfs/en/essentials_of_hindutva.v001.pdf, p. 17, accessed 15 January 2016.

11 http://www.savarkar.org/content/pdfs/en/
essentials_of_hindutva.v001.pdf, p. 17, accessed 15
January 2016.

Chapter 7

1 Ryot: A tenant farmer.
2 Panjurli: A popular bhoota in coastal Karnataka.

Chapter 8

1 Anthony J. Parel (edited, introduced and annotated
by), *Gandhi: 'Hind Swaraj' and Other Writings*,
Cambridge University Press, Cambridge, 1997.
2 Vishwaroopa: The all-pervading, all-including form
of the Lord.

Chapter 9

1 http://www.sacred-texts.com/tao/taote.htm
2 Sarvodaya: The social and economic development
of a community as a whole, or the upliftment of all,
a phrase coined by Mahatma Gandhi.
3 Chaturopaya: A four-fold political theory of peace
(sama), charity (dana), division (bheda) and force
(danda).
4 Anthony J. Parel (edited, introduced and annotated
by), *Gandhi: 'Hind Swaraj' and Other Writings*,
Cambridge University Press, Cambridge, 1997.

5   The Kannada writer and Jnanapith awardee Masti
    Venkatesha Iyengar.
6   Statism: The belief that the state should control
    either economic or social policy, or both, to some
    degree. It is effectively the opposite of Gandhi's
    anarchism.

Chapter 10

1   https://docs.google.com/document/
    d/1qFsSho6YFpkNRFjrUdn0sjV_pI_
    jfUyamVtn1hsbOAM/edit?hl=en_US, accessed on
    22 February 2016.
2   Ibid.

Epilogue

1   Maryada Purushottama: One who observes the
    noblest and finest traditions of a particular age or
    society.

Acknowledgements

The task of translating U.R. Ananthamurthy's last work was daunting. What gave us the courage to embark on it was the support we had from:

Namita Gokhale, who set the book on its journey;

Karthika V.K., Shantanu Ray Chaudhuri and Antony Thomas of HarperCollins;

Shiv Visvanathan who agreed to write the foreword with no persuasion;

Sheldon Pollock and Ashis Nandy who provided the blurb;

Srikanth Shastri, Sharath Ananthamurthy, who cast their discerning eyes over the translation and provided invaluable feedback, and Mukunda Shanbhag who participated in our discussions;

Ajitha G.S. for her patient, gentle prodding and meticulous reading which helped us make the text smoother;

the team at HarperCollins for the cover design, layout and production support.

To all of them a huge thank you.

We also thank Pattabhiram Somayaji who wanted so much to see this book in English.

Thanks also to Githa Hariharan for publishing an extract of this book in indianculturalforum.in.

About the Author

U.R. Ananthamurthy was one of the most influential voices of Kannada and Indian literature. Among the numerous awards and recognitions he received were the Jnanpith, Padma Bhushan, the Sahitya Akademi fellowship, the Basava award and a nomination for the Man Booker International Prize. One of the pioneers of the Navya movement, he is best known for his novels *Samskara and Bharatipura*. He is the author of six novels, as well as several short-story collections, poems, plays and essays. Until the end, URA, as he was affectionately known, remained a strong critic of India's shift to the non-secular right. He died on 22 August 2014 and remains deeply mourned. *Hindutva or Hind Swaraj* was his very last work.

About the Translators

Keerti Ramachandra is a teacher, editor and a translator from Kannada, Marathi and Hindi. Her translation, *A Dirge for the Dammed* (Vishwas Patil, Marathi) was shortlisted for the Crossword prize in 2015. She has received the Katha A.K. Ramanujan award (1995) and the Katha award (1997, 2000).

Vivek Shanbhag writes in Kannada. He has published five short-story collections, three novels and two plays, and edited two anthologies, one of which is in English. His novel *Ghachar Ghochar* (Harper Perennial, 2015) was published in translation to great acclaim. Vivek founded and edited the pioneering Kannada literary journal *Desha Kaala* for seven years. He is an engineer by training, and lives in Bangalore.